A Dancer's World

ALSO BY MARGOT FONTEYN IN STAR

Autobiography

A Dancer's World

AN INTRODUCTION

MARGOT FONTEYN

A STAR BOOK
published by
the Paperback Division of
W. H. ALLEN & Co. Ltd

To the memory of
GRACE BOSUSTOW
my first dancing teacher

A Star Book
Published in 1980
by the Paperback Division of
W. H. Allen & Co. Ltd
A Howard and Wyndham Company
44 Hill Street, London WIX 8LB

First published in Great Britain by
W. H. Allen & Co. Ltd, 1978

Copyright © Southern Maid Ltd, 1978

Printed in Great Britain
by W & J Mackay Limited, Chatham

ISBN 0 352 304413

Author's Acknowledgements

I would like to express my warmest thanks to Mrs Patricia M. Mackenzie, BB, ARAD, and to Miss Valerie Taylor, ARAD, of the Royal Academy of Dancing, and to Mr Terry Westmoreland of the Royal Ballet for their very helpful suggestions and comments.

The photographs have been chosen to give an impression rather than a direct illustration of the subject matter.

PHOTOGRAPHIC ACKNOWLEDGEMENTS

The author and publisher would like to thank the following collections and private individuals by whose kind permission the illustrations are reproduced. Sources without parentheses indicate the owners of photographs; those within parentheses refer to illustration sources only.

Page
11 Nadia Nerina in *Dragon Fly* – Houston Rogers
12 Margot Fonteyn in *Les Sylphides* – Felix Fonteyn
14 Monica Mason in *Prince Igor* – Roy Round
18 Young children in class – Felix Fonteyn
20 Early training – Felix Fonteyn
24 A teacher with students – Felix Fonteyn
28 Doreen Wells in *Pineapple Poll* – Royal Ballet
32 Young girl in national costume – Felix Fonteyn
37 Anthony Dowell – Royal Ballet
38 Student at Royal Academy of Dancing – Jennie Walton
41 Student at Royal Ballet School – Anthony Crickmay

Contents

Introduction

The world of dance is a charmed place. Some people like to inhabit it, others to behold it, either way it is rewarding. Those who look in from the outside are the spectators who love the beauty, the colours, the music, the drama and the physical prowess of the dancers. The more they see, the more they enjoy the great moments of excitement in the theatre and discover the small moments of grace and the tiny vignettes of acting.

It is a world that takes hold of its observers in an unusual way, by presenting some aspects of the universal ideal with which they momentarily identify as the dancers make their kaleidoscopic patterns over the stage.

For those who live in this magic world it has an even stronger hold. Life has an extra dimension of expression, wordless but powerful. If we limit our means of communication to the mind and head we need to have very rare minds of the kind that contain such a wealth of resources, in knowledge and abilities, that all their energies can be deployed in thinking.

Many of us do not have such minds but our bodies help us in expressing our emotions. Without counting the Italian race, who have such a spectacular language of the hands with which to emphasise their conversation, almost everyone makes use of gesture to accentuate a point of speech. Public speakers are among the best examples. Dancing carries the development of this physical expression to ultimate limits. It is by no means just a series of exercises and gymnastics, but an art in which no two performers are identical because each one puts into it something of himself, his very soul.

I am not talking only of stage performances, but of any kind of dancing no matter how unpretentious. The world of dance is a natural world from which civilisation has divorced many of us and has made it appear remote – something reserved for the few who have a special talent. That is because we associate dancing more with theatre than with the daily round of living and religious rites in which it was originally employed. The soul then was very much involved in the dance. It is not surprising that a primitive tribesman who witnessed European social dancing late in the last century expressed his disgust with the frivolous purpose for which it was used by white people. In fact, by setting dance somewhat apart from normal life we only waste a valuable aspect of living.

There are many ways in which we can exploit the gift of dance. I have tried to show all the possibilities and how they can best be located. It would be impossible to list dancing academies unless one instituted a kind of Michelin Guide, like the one for restaurants, with quality ratings reviewed annually. I am not in favour of such a project. My purpose is not only to make known the choices but to emphasise that the decisions are all personal, for each individual is different, each case is different and I would recommend readers to go through the book carefully, then put it down and follow their intelligence and instinct.

In addition to some guide-lines on approaching dance as a theatre art, it is intended that the book should open doors for all those interested in uniting mind and body in the most comprehensive means of expression and communication. Lack of communication among people is one of the sources of evil in our world. Let us consider dance not as a rare vocation, but as a blessing granted to all who have the inclination to enjoy it.

Part One

Dance   Move with rhythmical steps, glides, leaps, revolutions, gestures, etc., usually to music, alone or with a partner or set. Jump about, skip, move in lively way.

CONCISE OXFORD DICTIONARY

1. Dancing

One of the best things to be said about dancing is that like all the arts there is really no end to it. Therefore it is always interesting and no sooner has one learnt one thing than one realises how much more there is still to know; and with each lesson a little progress only opens up more possibilities.

Of course it is easy to lose enthusiasm for a pursuit that seems too difficult. On the other hand, there is always the chance to improve and that is a great attraction; for, generally speaking, we are all happier when we are still striving for achievement than when the prize is in our hands. And, in the case of working on the stage, even when we hold the prize it is only for a fleeting moment – a few short hours of performance and the cascade of applause at the end. But the next performance must be fought for and won all over again.

There is nothing better for children than an absorbing interest; they have such restless little minds and it keeps them out of mischief – for a while at least. The arts are perfect for that because they are eternal. I sometimes wonder if art is not meant for children, or whether there is not an artist lurking in every child. Those who have more pressing abilities or vocations to develop leave the artist in them in abeyance, or even forget about it as they grow up; whereas those who become artists continue to see life with some of the fantasy of childhood – which forms a kind of protective barrier around their sensibilities.

When considering the arts for children one can only give them all the options. Dancing, if the child should have some feeling for it, is more communal than painting or music. The pianist practises alone,

15

and drawing or painting are individual pursuits not dependent on others. But dancers work together, always conscious of each other and often subordinating their efforts to the unity of the whole.

It is almost impossible to turn dancing into anything malevolent or really unpleasant or even mean. So the practice of dancing brings people together in a friendly spirit. How much easier it is to have an argument in words than in dance; yet two dancers at a party or a night club are certainly in communication even if they don't say a word to each other.

In a way dance is a language without words, so there is communication and contact among the participants through their relationships in lines, circles or groups. Each step has its direction and pattern, making dancing a well-ordered occupation with well-defined rules. And what a relief that can sometimes be in a life so full of choices and decisions! I think children like to know exactly what is expected of them because they are basically logical and hate a lot of uncertainty and confusion.

To the minds of most people in the modern world, dancing classes are the province of children – little girls in particular – and of a special breed of people who are professional dancers. If we look back a little in history, however, we find that dancing was an obligatory social accomplishment in the seventeenth and eighteenth centuries, and 'the dancing lesson' was a necessary feature of life for all adults of the upper levels of society.

Surprisingly, the steps that those gentlemen dancing masters in satin knee breeches, lace ruffles and periwigs were so busy teaching to the golden youth of Europe in their day were, in many cases, the very same steps that little girls in pink tights, leotards and neatly pinned hair are now learning in their thousands all across the world from China to Peru. The *chassé*, *coupé* and *pirouette* are not inventions of a rarified world of modern ballet, but simply the steps of that old and dignified dance of the ballroom, the minuet. So let us not think of ballet and dance as pastimes far removed from the lives of ordinary mortals. Dance has always been, and always will be, a very basic form of human expression and communication.

2. Children

Everyone asks at what age children should start dancing lessons. In fact the choice of teacher is more important than the age of the pupil. Full ballet training, for example, is not recommended before nine or ten years old, but children's classes with a responsible teacher can be started from five on. Lessons could be once a week and there would definitely be no dancing on the toes.

Ballet classes for children up to the ages of ten or twelve provide something for everyone the slender, the lumpy, the gawky, the clumsy and the talented alike. In the last case they are also a preparation for professional training but should be regarded as specifically designed for children – and children are not 'ballerinas'. The idea of an infant prodigy used to be appealing to some parents, but it is definitely not encouraged in the world of professional ballet where even the stars are basically part of a uniform group

The world of dance is not comparable to the acting world in which there are roles that require actual children with appropriate voices. Most 'children' in ballet are danced by adult artists. So a young child going to ballet class would learn only the basic positions and exercises, and elementary steps combined in simple little dances to be performed at the annual school display. Without the child realising it, this work gives a sense of physical co-ordination. It serves admirably for sports and games, as well as exercising the mind in an effort of concentration completely different to that required for school studies.

Ballet is by no means the only type of dance for young children, but I talk about it more fully because it is the most complex, and because

the field of ballet schools is also rather complex for the parent wanting to give a child the best opportunity at the right age.

Where young children are concerned I do not believe it is necessary or right to over-emphasise the difficulties of ballet training. I mean that, when I was a child, no-one ever told me 'you will have to be prepared to work hard and be very dedicated if you want to become a ballerina'. If they had, I am sure it would have put me off. Luckily my mother took me to a good teacher who made the lessons enjoyable and interesting, so my dancing thrived.

It is rather important for mothers to understand that it is not in their power to make prodigies, stars or anything else. Their children are what they are and no amount of ambition or determination on the parent's part will alter the facts. If the child has talent there is no need for a 'pushy' parent, and if it has no talent there is nothing to be done, except to realise it. There is no sense in imposing a burden on the child which it cannot live up to.

When I was young there was no kind of pressure involved. If I entered for an examination or a competition, or if I was to dance in a school display, there was a lot of excitement in the preparation – and I was even unconsciously nervous, but that was all part of the fun. It was interesting, but never too serious. Above all I think dancing should be a happy affair. It is, after all, the most spontaneous expression of elation. 'Jumping for joy' is a very basic human reaction, and a child hop-skipping down the street is simply an untrained dancer.

3. Early Training

With dancing, perhaps more than any other art, there is no question that the single most important factor is a good teacher. It is very discouraging to find after several years of training that one is doing everything wrong, and in addition that it takes more time to put the fault right than it would have done to learn properly in the first place. This is because the limbs themselves have to know what to do – and they learn far more slowly than the brain. If one tries to correct a movement which has been wrongly taught the body has to unlearn what it was doing and start all over again – a double process. This is a silly waste of time and effort – to be avoided if at all possible.

There are, for example, certain elementary rules in ballet which should be learnt correctly from the first day. The most important concerns the stance, sometimes referred to by that even more comically Victorian word 'posture'. It means that the child should stand up straight with head erect, spine vertical and shoulders down – no slumping, sagging, or bulging.

So far no great problem, but then comes the 'turn out'. 'Turn out' is generally thought of as turning the feet so that the toes are out to the sides instead of to the front. But it is not just the feet that must turn, but the whole leg from the hip joint.

This turn out is the most difficult part of early training. Each child is constructed differently, some have loose hip joints, others have a very restricted range of movement. Teachers have to assess what is right for each child. The common fault is to turn the feet further than the knees and hips, which results in what is called 'rolling over on the ankles'.

A Dancer's World

The best way to judge how far the feet can turn out to the sides is by bending the knees, and, as long as they are *above* the toes (not more to the front), it is correct *provided* that the spine is straight and vertical. In other words, anyone can get it right by letting the bottom stick out but that is no good.

If, to test the position, the whole back is held flat against a wall, with the heels almost touching the wall too, and then the knees bend *above* the toes of the turned out feet (the shoulders and back sliding gently down the wall), it is easy to judge how far the hip joint will turn naturally. If the feet are too far out the knees can no longer bend above the toes but will move forward and pull the ankles forward with them so that they are 'rolling over'.

What is wrong with 'rolling over' is that the *whole* sole of the foot is no longer in firm contact with the floor, and it is that contact which is the most valuable thing a dancer has. From that use of the floor comes stability, control and, most important of all, the power to spring up into the air. If, for example, an arrow is bent or crooked it loses speed and cannot fly as it would if it were straight. Similarly, a dancer jumping in the air is like a crooked arrow if the push off comes from a 'rolled over' ankle. To make a really good arrow, of course, the knees must be very braced and straight too.

Again, if a chair or table has one leg slightly shorter than the other we all know it will wobble as soon as weight is put on that corner. It is rather the same for a person trying to stand on one turned out leg with the other raised high. If *all* the sole of the foot is evenly on the floor they will balance well, but if the ankle is rolling over and most of the weight is on that forward side of the foot they will be wobbly.

The important thing, therefore, even in a beginners' class, is care and attention to stance and turn out. At first the legs are turned out as far as they can go, naturally without the danger of ankles rolling and, very gradually, as a little strength is developed in the muscles, the hips are turned a bit further; however, some children will never have a good turn out because their physical construction will not permit it. It is dangerous to *force* even the more supple ones because their bones are growing and are consequently still soft.

The question of when a student should first have toe shoes is one on

which it is better to be safe than sorry. The answer is 'not before the feet are prepared to take the strain' which might be around thirteen years old and, even then, only after about three years of serious training.

Some types of physique are more vulnerable to strain in early training than others and a good teacher these days is expected to have an adequate knowledge of anatomy. One cannot be too careful with young children.

Do not be misled by pictures of Russian children standing strongly on their toes with straight legs and tightly braced knees at the age of ten. Those are the ones specially selected from among thousands and subjected to a rigorous physical examination before being chosen for professional training. Even so, there is a difference of opinion about the necessity of acquiring so much mastery so young. England's Royal Ballet School develops the children far more slowly but produces equally good dancers in the end.

From all this one can see just how advisable it is to go to a good teacher in the first place. 'If a thing is worth doing, it is worth doing well', my grandmother used to say, and to my mind they are words of eternal truth.

4. Teachers

You may well ask, 'How do I find a good teacher?' to which there is no very easy answer. Of course, if you live in a small town you may not have a choice, you must trust to luck with your only local dancing school. Nevertheless, you could make some useful observations and do a bit of research.

Apart from my explanations of stance and turn out, which might be a bit difficult to understand at first, there are some general observations you could make which, when all added together, would help in the assessment of your teacher, such as:

* Does she have authority and assurance when teaching?
* Does she insist on pupils being neatly dressed (and is she neatly dressed herself)?
* Does she hold the attention of the class, or are the younger ones running about chattering and out of control?
* Does she generally give a lot of corrections or just show the steps and let the pupils get on as best they can?
* Does she try to vary the lesson from time to time, or does she mechanically repeat the same exercises at each class?
* Does she demonstrate the movements carefully and take trouble over getting them right, or does she seem to think that limbering and high kicks are all that matter?
* Does she have some good common sense?

Without being either over-dramatic or plain boring, a teacher should somehow manage to get the serious concentration of her pupils. They will then respond with that little bit of extra effort to get something right, and she should follow it with a word of encouragement when they are successful.

A teacher who continually gives little individual corrections inspires more attention from her pupils than the one who only addresses the whole class occasionally with a blanket comment. One who gives almost no corrections at all is not giving true value – although it is fair to remember that a big class of young beginners is almost too much for one person to handle. Some teachers use the assistance of senior students to correct the tiny children so that each one gets some individual help.

I have tried earlier to explain exactly what is meant by technical terms like 'turn out' and 'rolling ankles' because technique provides the foundation on which the ballet dancer's final accomplishment is built – just as a house must have a solid basis of support or it will always be insecure. But the kind of house that is built on that foundation is quite another matter, open to endless possibilities. It could be purely functional, lacking in style or even ugly; it could be charming to look at, having graceful lines; it could be an efficient building but without any special interest; it could be a noble and beautiful mansion of perfect proportions; or it could have some special individual features of its own.

And so also with the dancer; what matters is what is built on the foundation. The technique is only there to allow the fullest control and the fullest range of movement, but the movement alone is not enough, it is merely exercise – the efficient house of no special interest. From that point, the artist – or architect – goes forward into personal expression in the creation of his art. With a developed technique the dancer is able to express emotional and dramatic situations or pure grace and beauty in movement.

It may seem premature to look so far ahead when talking of teachers for young children, but every good teacher has an innate sense of what dance really means. She does not teach it in any precise way, she imparts it because it is somewhere in her own movements as she demonstrates to the children. They absorb it as children absorb every-thing the teacher has to give them.

Generally speaking, I do not think it is too difficult to recognise a good teacher when you find one, it is just that it would be wise to look around and be sure you have the best that is available.

The dance magazines offer a lot of information by way of adver-tisements and reports on various schools but, of course, it is pure information requiring a certain amount of deduction to distinguish between the good and the merely adequate. In the end trial and error might be the best way to decide among two or three alternatives.

I think all teachers these days attend conference weeks or various refresher courses held by the dance teachers' organisations of different countries. After all, no one teaches badly except out of ignorance, and we all know that there is never any end to learning.

5. Local Dance Schools

Local dancing schools vary enormously in the types of dance they offer. Broadly speaking, the schools fall into three groups. One would specialise in 'stage dancing' as required for musicals and commercial theatre, TV and films etc., which includes jazz, tap and modern dance. Many such schools now offer ballet classes as well because so many basically ballet trained dancers work in this field of stage dancing.

However, a student hoping to find a place in a ballet company would look for the type of school that definitely specialises in ballet. Such a school might also teach modern dance, and possibly Spanish or other alternative forms.

The third group is that of schools specialising in modern dance on the highest level. They do not normally offer a variety of other styles. The directors of these schools have trained in one of the well known systems of modern dance such as Martha Graham or Lester Horton. The technique is very different from ballet and must be studied just as seriously.

In the case of the specialist ballet schools many are directed by professional dancers of high standing, whose long experience on the stage gives them unique knowledge. Such teachers have their own individual contribution to give their pupils. It is based on their personal attributes as performers, and each one is different. It is in this very personal way that the art of ballet has been handed down from generation to generation for three hundred years. The older artists help to develop the young, not just in the exercises and technique but in their presentation on stage. The steps learnt in school are merely

29

the alphabet of movement; when they are linked together in a ballet there are a thousand different ways in which they can be made significant, just as words or phrases can be made clumsy or poetic according to the way they are spoken. It is the ability to convey these nuances that makes a true artist.

There are also many first-rate teachers who have not been great dancers on the stage. They often understand and inspire the younger children and have perhaps more patience with them. Teaching is a different talent to that of performing; the two do not necessarily go together in the same person. Each teacher should be taken finally on his or her own merits, and in relation to the point of development the student has reached.

Studio premises can present problems for the local ballet teacher. In many cities it is difficult, or prohibitively expensive, to find suitably spacious accommodation and equip it with the right flooring, *barres** and mirrors. For small children some compromise arrangement is adequate but it is never desirable to use the back of a chair for support instead of a properly secured rail, and serious students do need a proper studio. It need not be enormous but should have a non-slippery floor surface, either wood or linoleum, which ideally should not be laid directly on concrete as that is bad for the muscles. The *barres* should be either fixed to the walls or else portable *barres*, well steadied by weights. Mirrors are a necessity for senior students.

Last but not least, a word about music. A surprising number of dancers are quite unmusical and some teachers too – partly because so much attention has to go into doing the steps that little is left over to concentrate on fitting them to the music. There was a time when it would have been unthinkable to have a dance class without a pianist, but the economics of small private businesses today make a pianist a luxury at the very least, sometimes an impossibility.

It is a sad fact that many teachers are forced to use taped music. No matter how fine the recording, there remains something impersonal about it and it makes less demand upon the student to use his or her ears.

* These are rails fixed to the wall at about elbow-height.

It is hard to advise on the type of dance school to go for; I think ballet is the safest first choice when there is doubt, because it is easier to go from ballet into stage dancing or modern than the reverse. Also the quality of stage dancing is considerably higher and its artistic value greater now that ballet is so popular and has had a considerable influence on it.

If choosing a stage dancing school, look for the same happy atmosphere that is desirable in all dance classes. A will to work on the part of the children is good, and the competitive spirit is fine too, but not when it takes the joy out of dance.

Dance is essentially an art that gives health and happiness and it should not be allowed to breed evil jealousies, bad character or nervous breakdowns. The old stories of rivals – either the dancers or their mothers – slashing costumes and putting glass in each other's shoes before the show might be true for all I know, but they have nothing to do with art. And art is the most satisfying element in any type of dancing whether in sparkling musicals, grand ballets or significant modern innovations.

6. Examinations

While on the subject of the independent local schools, it is worth noting that there are one or two important dance organisations that hold examinations – principally in ballet – in many parts of the world. The exams are open to pupils of any school that will prepare them in the set syllabus and enter sufficient candidates to make the examiner's visit viable. They approximate roughly to examinations in music.

The point of these examinations is two-fold; first, that they really examine the teachers – because a pupil's performance is the result of the teacher's ability. A pupil with bad faults is the product of an ignorant teacher. Secondly, the examinations assess the abilities of the child or student in relation to others of his or her approximate age group elsewhere, perhaps in larger cities or even other countries.

The examinations serve as a yardstick for students, parents, and teachers to measure how they stand generally in the whole field of dance training, and in this context have an unarguable value. However, it has to be understood that they are only a test; the exam does not make the dancer, it only assesses, and the certificate is not a passport to employment. No-one engages a dancer purely on the basis of his or her credits on paper. To get a job the dancer must be seen dancing and each ballet company tends towards a preference for a particular type of dancer.

These examinations are usually divided into two groups, for young children and for teenage students respectively. The examinations for small children are very short – ten to twenty minutes – and for advanced students an hour at least. The system of marking and certificates varies with each organisation; also the syllabuses and markings are updated from time to time.

One should know that the markings in the children's group of exams are not, and certainly should not be, set to any 'professional' standard. That is to say that a high result for a child of ten or twelve, for example, would not necessarily indicate that you have a future ballerina on your hands, although in rare cases you just might. It would mean, however, that she is above average and you would be justified in moving her on to serious student training. The difference between a child with good examination results and a serious student is about the same as that between a big fish in a small pool and a little sprat in the ocean. There is never any harm in trying to make the transition but it is a good idea to keep an open mind and not to expect too much.

7. Ballet and General Education

Apart from the specialist local ballet schools there are schools that give a full general education as well as full ballet training. The reason for combined schools is obvious: it is so much easier to fit dancing into the schedule of general education if both take place in the same school. Economically it is not so easy because it requires a double staff. The arrangement varies according to the subsidy – if any – that is available. For example, students of the Russian theatre schools, which are entirely state supported, can be resident from their acceptance until graduation eight years later with full academic tuition.

In most European opera houses, also subsidised, the pupils attend for general education and ballet but live at home. The Royal Ballet School in London – partially subsidised – has a resident Junior School, and a non-resident Senior School to complete the dance training after school-leaving age. The American Ballet Theatre School in New York is part-subsidised, non-resident and non-educational, but gives a full ballet training at both Junior and Senior levels. All these schools are attached to ballet companies and the best graduates are taken into the companies whenever there are vacancies. Their training in the school gives them a necessary unity of style. There are also a few combined schools run on a normal commercial basis in England and the United States and some in Europe.

The normal age for entry to a Junior School is nine or ten years. Even at that age a child with bad faults might find them hard to eradicate. In such circumstances the school would give preference to a child with no previous training at all.

Some parents feel considerable concern as to what will happen if their child *is* accepted into the combined ballet and general education school, knowing that eventual employment in a ballet company is by no means assured. They wonder whether the standard of general education leaves something to be desired and failure in the dancing field will leave the student at graduation neither balletically nor academically ready for employment. On this question the parents should be reassured that the schools make special efforts to maintain a normal academic standard at the very least. There is the example of the daughter of a famous English ballerina who entered the Royal Ballet School as a child, studied there until the age of sixteen, then decided that her vocation was not in dance but medicine. She progressed to a university, medical school with excellent results and has settled happily into her chosen profession as a fully-qualified doctor.

Nevertheless one must consider the problem of selection, because there are usually many more applicants that there are places. Failure is a more shattering disappointment than it would be in the case of entry to a purely academic school in which case there would be several alternatives, and dancing would be a continuing study at the local dance school. Failure to enter the specialist combined school causes a big crisis of discouragement; yet the child is only ten! The selection has been made mainly on physical suitability, and although other children may have better backs, legs and feet, they may have less real feeling for dance which is a more nebulous quality.

An alternative system which seems to work well is that of the Australian Ballet School (attached to the Australian Ballet Company), which is a Senior School only. In that country where there are excellent local ballet teachers in every state, the selection for the professional school comes at fifteen or sixteen and some very fine dancers have graduated from the school. The secret lies in the quality of teaching that the students can get before they enter the school attached to a ballet company. I believe that the 'local' ballet schools have certain advantages but they also have a tremendous responsibility and their teachers need to be very intelligent and enlightened to meet the challenge. That they are able to do so has been proved beyond doubt in Australia and by some excellent teachers in various other countries.

8. Boys

For boys it is strongly advisable to enter a school of ballet and general education as young as possible, because it is so difficult for them to combine any kind of dance classes with an ordinary school schedule – and boys need the early training. Wherever there are opportunities for boys to get good daily ballet lessons from ten or twelve years old there are superb male dancers. No longer are they the sole prerogative of Russia and Denmark; many other countries are now in the field and have produced international stars.

When I say that boys need the early training it might sound as though it is more necessary for them than for girls. In fact both are put at a disadvantage for professional ballet if they start too late. It is not a question, as I believe is the case with acrobats, of having to start in extreme youth but, if one discounts the once-a-week children's classes which serve as a preparation only, eight to ten is a good age to start ballet, twelve is still alright and after that each year is more disadvantageous than the last.

It is more difficult for boys than for girls because their muscles and tendons are stronger and harder, so the sooner they start the long labour of learning to move in certain patterns the better, and every bit of training facilitates co-ordination by making the muscles more responsive. To respond quickly they must be familiar with the movements required of them and in condition to perform them instantly; the tendons, too, must be as supple as possible to avoid any chance that a sudden movement will cause over-strain.

A fully professional dancer performing several times a week and training daily will feel his muscles so finely in tune that even one day off – a free Sunday – leaves him feeling that he has not practised for a week. After forty minutes or so of exercise his control returns and he is back in top form. A week without any dancing means another week before he is back at his peak and a month must be paid for with a month of re-training.

A young man whose physique is fully developed and his bones already adult when he starts his training has to work with much less amenable material than, say, a twelve-year-old boy, who is still in the process of formation. The finest male dancers move with the power and control of a tiger; they can spring into the air, twist and turn their bodies and limbs and land gently with absolute precision. There is no visible trace of the effort involved.

Traditionally male dancers are divided into three types according to their physique. First, the *danseur noble* who has elegant proportions, long legs and a noble bearing. He dances principal roles and is expected to have control in slow movements which display the harmony of his line; he never makes a jerky movement or an ugly position but dances all the steps with grace and ease, even the most difficult pirouettes and leaps.

The second type is the *demi-character* dancer, a little more compact in physique than the *danseur noble*, and his dances are quicker in order to show off his brilliant footwork, bounding jumps and fast turns.

The third type was originally called *comique* – or even *grotesque* – when the ballets were mostly about mythological subjects including various fantastic creatures or beasts. These dancers are now called *character dancers*. They are of stocky build, never very tall, and they do all kinds of national dances and character or comic parts.

Men who rise to fame in the dance world are like a small aristocracy. Although actors can be counted in thousands, dancers are only numbered in hundreds, and the finest among them are less than a dozen. With them lies the future of dance for, with a few exceptions, men are the creators, they carry dance forward into new fields of invention and give it new life.

Dance definitely holds as much scope for men as for women – probably more so. The history of ballet was started by dancing masters who established the first principles and wrote the first books on technique. For a short period when men dropped almost completely out of ballet it very nearly died. Luckily they are now securely back again and hold a highly honoured position in the arts. Sir Frederick Ashton, England's greatest choreographer, holds the Companion of Honour, one of the highest honours that the Queen can bestow upon her subjects.

9. Translation of Some French Terms Used in Ballet

Ballet dancing in its present form is derived directly from the first professional school and ballet company established in 1669, in Paris. The names of the steps are therefore all in French. Even in the seventeenth century they were not new but were terms used in the social dancing of the day. They described steps developed by the Italian and French dance teachers over a century and more; the origins of some steps lay in ethnic folk dances. So even when professional ballet training was inaugurated, it employed time-worn steps.

With the passing of three hundred years the usage of some movements has evolved considerably and so has the usage of the French language. Add to that the fact that French ballet terminology has been used world-wide, often by people with the scantiest knowledge of the French language, and you will understand why there are inconsistencies and confusions in its use and interpretation.

Without explaining the steps that bear these different French names, I am putting down dictionary translations into English of some commonly used ballet terms. Italics indicate the interpretation that is closest to their application to dance.

ADAGIO	(music) adagio, *slow* time
AIR	air (*en l'air – in the air*)
ALLÉGRO	(music) *brisk* time
ALLONGÉ	*lengthened, elongated*
APLOMB	*equilibrium*, perpendicularity, *assurance*, self-command, self-possession

43

ARRIÈRE	*behind (en arrière de – behind)*
ASSEMBLÉ	*assembled*, united, joined
ATTITUDE	*attitude*, posture, *pose*
AVANT	*forward (en avant de – in front of)*
BALANCÉ	to balance, to poise, *to swing*, to wave, *to rock*, to counter-balance
BALANÇOIRE	*see-saw*
BALLON	balloon, *india-rubber ball*
BALLONÉ	distended, swollen
BALLOTTÉ	tossed, *tossed about*, kept in suspense, *bandied (a tennis ball)*
BARRE	bar, rod, *rail* (of metal, wood, etc.), wooden batten
BAS	*low*
BATTEMENT	clapping (of hands), stamping (of feet), *flapping (of wings)*, beating (of the heart), shuffling (of cards)
BATTERIE	fight, scuffle, rough and tumble, *beat (of drum)*, roll *(on side drum)*, *quick succession of notes*
BATTU	*beaten*, fought
BOURRÉE	old French dance in 3/4 time
BRAS	*arms*
BRISÉ	*broken*, folded
CABRIOLE	*leap*, caper, goat's leap, somersault
CAMBRÉ	*bent*, *arched*, well-set
CHANGEMENT	*change*, alteration of course
CHAT	*cat*
CHASSÉ	*chased*, pursued, hunted
CHEVAL	*horse*
CISEAUX	*scissors*
CLOCHE	*bell*
CONTRETEMPS	note played, *step danced against the beat*, on the unaccented portion of the beat, out of time
CORPS	body, *organised body* of men
CORYPHÉE	Coryphaeus, *leader of the chorus*, *leader of the ballet*

CÔTÉ	*side* (*de côté* – *sideways*)
COU	*neck*
COU-DE-PIED	*instep*
COUPÉ	*cut*, cut up, broken up, jerky style
COURONNE	*crown, coronet*, wreath
COURU	ran, *running*
CROISÉ	*crossed*
CROIX	*cross* (*en croix* – *crosswise*)
CUISSE	*thigh*
DE	*of, for*, by
DEBOULÉ	*rolled* (*like a ball*)
DÉBUT	*first appearance*, beginning
DEDANS	within, *in*, inside (*en dedans* – *inwards*)
DÉGAGÉ	*disengaged*, redeemed, flippant, bold, easy
DEHORS	*out*, without, outside (*en dehors* – *outwards*)
DEMI	*half*
DERRIÈRE	*behind*
DESSOUS	*under*
DESSUS	*over*
DÉTOURNÉ	*turned away*, retired, oblique
DEVANT	*front*
DÉVELOPPÉ	opened, unwrapped, *unfolded*, developed, expanded
DIVERTISSEMENT	*diversion*, amusement, *entertainment*, recreation
DOS	*back*, rear
DOUBLÉ	*doubled*
DROÎTE	right (*à droîte* – *to the right*)
ECARTÉ	set aside, removed, waived, passed over, dispelled, *widened*
ECHAPPÉ	*escaped*, run away
EFFACÉ	effaced, expunged, rubbed out, thrown into the shade (*s'effacer* – to draw aside, *to give way, to turn the body sideways*)
ELANCÉ	launched, *darted*, shot
EMBOÎTE	jointed, set, *fitted, fitted in*
EN	*in*, into, within, on, *to, at, like*

ENCHAÎNMENT	chain, *series, logical sequence*
ENCHAÎNER	to chain up, enchain, *to link, to correct*
ENTRECHAT	caper, cross capers
ENTRÉE	*entrance, entry, entering, coming in,* reception, beginning, introduction
ENTRELACÉ	interwined, interlaced, interwoven
ENVELOPPÉ	*enveloped, wrapped up,* covered, folded up
EPAULÉE	*push (with the shoulder),* shouldering
EPAULEMENT	a shoulder-piece, covert, *shoulder*
EQUILIBRE	*balance, equilibrium, poise*
ETOILE	*star*
FACE	*front, (de face de – in front of, full face)* (*en face de* – in the face of, opposite)
FAILLI	*missed, failed,* trespassed, transgressed, mistaken
FERMÉ	*closed,* shut
FLÈCHE	*arrow,* dart, shaft
FONDU	*melted,* dissolved, *softened* (fondue – melted cheese)
FOUETTÉ	*whipped,* streaked (flowers), whipped (cream)
FRAPPÉ	*struck,* smitten, slapped, tapped, *hit*
GARGOUILLADE	a rattling, a rumbling, a dabbling, *a paddling*
GAUCHE	*left (à gauche – to the left)*
GLISSADE	*sliding,* slide, slipping, slip
GLISSÉ	*slide*
GRAND	great, large, *high,* lofty, tall, *wide, big, huge,* grand
HAUT	*high,* tall, (en haut – upstairs)
JAMBE	*leg,* shank
JETÉ	*thrown,* cast
LEVÉ	*lifted, raised up*
LIÉ	Bound, *tied,* friendly, intimate
MAILLOT	*tights,* fleshings, jersey
MAÎTRE	*master, (maître à danser* – dancing master, *maître de ballet* – ballet master)
MANÈGE	horsemanship, *manège, riding-school*
MARCHE	*walk, walking,* advance, step

OUVERT	*open*
PAS	*step,* pace, footstep (*pas de – step of*) (*pas seul –* solo; *pas de deux – dance for two; pas de trois –* dance for three, etc.; *pas de basque – à Basque* step, etc.)
PASSÉ	*passed*
PENCHÉ	bent, *leaning*
PETIT	*small, little,* diminutive, short
PIED	*foot*
PIQUÉ	*pricked,* stung
PIROUETTE	*rapid whirling round,* whirligig
PLIÉ	*folded, (bend of knee in dancing)*
POINTE	*point, (sur les pointes – on the toes)*
POINTÉ	*pointed*
POINTU	*pointed, sharp, peaked*
POISSON	*fish*
PORT	harbour, port, *carriage* (of parcels) presence, *bearing,* gait (*port de bras – carriage of the arms*)
PORTÉ	*carried,* inclined, prone, disposed
POSE	*posture, attitude*
POSÉ	*poised,* bearing, resting, leaning
POSER	*to place,* to set, to lay down
RACCOURCI	*shortened,* abbreviated
RAMASSÉ	*gathered up,* compact, clustered
RELEVÉ	*raised,* erect, high, exalted, refined
RENVERSÉ	*reversed, turned upside down*
RÉPÉTER	to repeat
RÉPÉTITION	repetition, *rehearsal*
RETIRÉ	retired, *withdrawn, contracted,* secluded
RÉVÉRENCE	reverence, *bow, curtsy*
ROND	*round,* ring, *circle,* disc
SAUT	*leap, jump,* skip, bound
SAUTÉ	*jumped*
SCÈNE	*scene,* stage
SERRÉ	*close,* compact, tight
SOUBRESAUT	sudden start, bound, leap (of horse, etc.)

SOUTENU	*sustained*, unremitting, unceasing, unfailing
TEMPS	*measure* (of music), beat, stress, accent
TENDU	*stretched*, strained, tense, taut, tight
TERRE	earth, land, *ground*, territory (*à terre – on the ground*)
TOMBÉ	*fallen*, fallen down, *dropped down*
TOUR	rotation, *turn*
TOURNANT	*turning*
VOLÉ	stolen, robbed, *taken away, flown, soared*

NUMBERS

Un, une	–	one
Deux	–	two
Trois	–	three
Quatre	–	four
Cinq	–	five
Six	–	six
Sept	–	seven
Huit	–	eight
Neuf	–	nine
Dix	–	ten
Onze	–	eleven
Douze	–	twelve

POSITIONS

Première	–	first
Seconde	–	second
Troisième	–	third
Quatrième	–	fourth
Cinquième	–	fifth

10. Ballet Shoes

Ballet shoes have no right or left feet. When they are new they are interchangeable until the dancer works them in and decides which goes best on which foot.

They should more accurately be called slippers, as they are derived from the light silk slippers worn by fashionable ladies to evening dances in the last century. The French still call them *chaussons* meaning slippers rather than *chaussures* meaning shoes. In English they are now universally called shoes.

There are soft ballet shoes and blocked, or point, shoes. The soft shoes are worn by boys and men. They are made in very light leather lined with canvas. The under sole is much smaller than the sole of the foot so that the dancer's toes and part of his heel stand on the soft upper leather which is turned back under the foot and pleated into the sole underneath the toes. The soles should be thin and very flexible so that the dancer can arch his instep and stretch his toes unimpeded by the shoe.

Girls wear the same soft shoes in either canvas or leather when they begin to learn simple children's dancing or ballet. If the shoes are too rigid the foot muscles cannot exercise properly and do not develop strength. The shoes should be flexible. In fact, they are best when they are old and have become pliant like a glove.

Point shoes (from *sur la pointe* in French meaning 'on the point' or standing on the points of the toes), are also called toe shoes. They are the same as soft shoes except that there is a small piece of leather between the outer and inner soles which gives support to the lower arch of the foot when standing on point, and the toe of the shoe is

reinforced with an extra layer of canvas hardened with paste. The point of the shoe is squared off so that there is a little flat area to balance on.

Ideally the shoes should be rather weak and the feet strong, but this situation is generally reversed for reasons of economy. Students cannot afford many shoes so they want a lot of wear from each pair, consequently the shoes are over-blocked and the soles – or backs – are almost rigid. As this prevents the foot muscles from exercising properly, the shoes do most of the work.

Professional dancers are accustomed to breaking their shoes down by any means, even hitting them with a hammer, until they reach a comfortable degree of pliancy.

Point shoes for use on the stage traditionally come in pink satin and are dyed to other colours by the wearer when so required. White satin – or even black – are sometimes available or can be specially ordered. The men's shoes are normally white, black or grey.

All ballet shoes have a little draw string that is tied at the centre front and the ends tucked inside. This is usually sufficient for the soft shoes to hold on while dancing but, if not, a piece of narrow elastic is stiched across the upper instep.

Point shoes have ribbons (one yard or one metre per shoe) which are crossed first in front of the ankle, then again at the back, then once more in the front, and finally tied just behind the inside ankle bone with the ends tucked away from sight. They are never tied in a bow.

Curiously, all ballet shoes are sold without either ribbons or elastics. These are a matter of personal preference and must be bought separately and stitched on by the dancer – or by the dancer's mother!

II. The Mother

The greatest assets one can possibly have in life are wise parents, and I was blessed with ones who made sacrifices to give me every opportunity yet always allowed me to feel that it was my career not theirs.

'Ballet Mother' was a term of dread to me when I was in my teens because certain other mothers had given all of them a dubious name. Happily mine never gave me a moment of embarrassment; she suffered my nerves worked off onto her as though she were a cushion; she always had a meal ready when I got home from long rehearsals; and stood by me with her sense of pride well under control and out of sight. What more could one ask?

RECOLLECTIONS OF A DANCER'S MOTHER

My daughter was born on 18th May, 1919. We christened her Margaret; she is now called Margot Fonteyn.

We lived in Ealing when I took her to her first ballet class. She was not yet five years old and I did so with no particular view to her becoming a professional dancer. Her father in fact suggested that the classes would be good for her deportment, which to me seemed an extraordinary word to use, because although when she was concentrating on a game or trying to read she would hunch her shoulders and screw up her eyes, her body was as straight as a young sapling and beautifully proportioned.

It was luck that the teacher we found, Miss Grace Bosustow, who lived round the corner from us, had the letters AOD after her name on a plate beside her gate – although I had no idea what the letters meant at the time.

When we went for an interview, I noticed that the front sitting room was slightly bigger than ours and had no furniture but a piano and a few small chairs. One wall had a large mirror, and the others had wooden poles attached to them about three feet from the floor. On one of those walls was a framed picture of a certificate awarded to Grace Bosustow by the Association of Operatic Dancing (now the Royal Academy of Dancing) which of course accounted for the letters after her name. This, to me, proved that she was a qualified teacher, and that Margot would be correctly trained, although I had no idea how important this would be in later years. As for me, I had absolutely no knowledge of classical ballet, I only knew that I loved dancing and that I admired grace and fluidity of movement.

Miss Bosustow was a charming woman, and we agreed that Margot should attend the classes for juniors every Friday afternoon. Margot loved them from the start and took it all very seriously, doing her best to do exactly what she was told. She first learnt the five positions of the feet and then to point her foot in front of her with the little toe on the ground.

Margot was a quick learner, a calm and determined student – qualities that are extremely important in a dancer, I believe. Miss Bosustow once wrote about Margot, 'From the first I thought she was a sweet little girl and very original. Though I don't think she was shy in the usual sense of the word, she seldom spoke unless spoken to, and would never say "yes" if a nod would do as well. Her manner was very grave and somehow remote. She was not at all vivacious, and everything she did was placid and determined.'

From my point of view, in the dancing class she always looked better than the other children, moved better, as any young animal does. Prejudice perhaps, but watching her against the others in later classes, she just looked different doing exactly the same movements. I always went along with Margot to her classes and watched – and learnt. In fact, we both learnt together, so that I also knew what each movement should be. This knowledge proved valuable, for when my husband's business called us abroad and we had to find new teachers,

I was able to recognise a good teacher from a bad one – and that is the best thing a parent can learn. I continued to watch for the next ten years.

The great snag these days is that most teachers do not allow parents to watch their children in class. They might get invited once a month, if they are lucky. Of course, many parents can be perfect nuisances. They become jealous, ambitious, and over-protective. The trouble is that a group of mothers with children all think that their child is the best, and in my way I did too, but I kept my mouth shut about it. Every teacher will tell you of the typical 'ballet mother' who babbles on about her child's talent, who criticises the teacher and the other children's ability, who literally thinks and talks as if the child and the parent were one and the same person.

This type of parent can only hinder a child's success in whatever he or she is doing. Children, especially young children, are very sensitive to their parents' feelings and the last thing a fledgling dancer needs is this kind of pressure. One of the most important things I have learnt in my life is to say very little. Think plenty, but say nothing.

These days, if your child wants to dance, you should encourage her. You must give her every opportunity. You must find the best accredited teacher you can, either by studying the dance magazines, which contain reams of information, or by finding out the name of the teacher who taught a dancer you particularly admire. You can do this through the magazines again, or by looking in any of the various dance encyclopedias.

Anyway, once you have chosen a teacher whom you respect, you must place all your faith in that teacher and in your child. There comes a point when you have to let your children go. They will either make a success or a flop – but at this stage, it is their responsibility, not yours. I let Margot go the day she was accepted into the Vic-Wells Ballet Company. She was then fourteen years old.

Each year, Miss Bosustow gave a prize to the child who had made the most progress, and Margot won it at the end of her first year. Then there were RAD (Royal Academy of Dancing) exams to take, when apart from showing the steps she had learnt, she had to answer questions about them. When we were at home I would say to Margot,

'What is a *plié*?' and she would promptly reply, 'It is a bending of the knees over the toes.' And then I would say, 'Oh, then what is a *grand battement*?' and again promptly, 'It's a throwing up of the leg from the hip' and so on. She remembered everything, but always the day before any exam or performance or competition she would get a temperature and have to stay in bed. Somehow she always managed to recover to do what she had to do. For her Grade I exam she got 95 out of 100 marks; Grade II the next year 85; Grade III, 70.

Margot, of course, was still very young. She loved dancing, that was obvious. She didn't much care for the hard work, but she loved performing and dressing up, and she seemed to understand that one was necessary for the other.

Miss Bosustow's classes were in no way advanced. She was a cheerful and encouraging teacher. She corrected her students gently, but firmly and never pushed a child beyond its limits.

After those three years, my husband's business dictated that we move to China, via the United States. We stayed in Louisville, Kentucky, for a time, and I enrolled Margot in a co-educational public school. She had difficulty making friends there, so it was not long before I started looking for a ballet school to supplement her education. I pursued this interest basically because it was clear that Margot loved it, and it was obviously something that she did well. By this time, she considered it a natural part of her life, although it never entered her head, or mine, that one day it would become her career.

I found only one school in the telephone directory, and when Margot and I went along to watch a class we were surprised by what we saw. First of all, there was very little discipline, and students of a similar age to Margot were involved in doing high kicks and splits. It was also clear that they hadn't learnt the basic ballet positions properly. I made up my mind then that no classes were better than bad classes.

Doubtless times have changed, and I am sure that one can now find reputable teachers in Louisville, or anywhere else for that matter. The fact remains, however, that it is still very easy to stumble onto a bad one.

From Kentucky we moved to Tientsin in China. There I was lucky to find a Russian lady called Madame Svetlanova who had a ballet school. Although the styles were different, her classes were very like those of Miss Bosustow and so Margot resumed her study. She was quite happy and enjoyed herself there.

At home we started to arrange dances ourselves to a portable gramophone we had brought from England. We spent a lot of time choosing suitable records. Before we left Margot got her first press notice for a tambourine dance she had made up herself. She was the hit of the performance and obviously gave it her all.

Later, after a brief visit back to London, we moved to Shanghai, and it was there that ballet for us became less of a pleasant pastime and more of a consuming interest.

I was, by then, a keen subscriber to the *Dancing Times*, Britain's leading dance magazine. It used to arrive every month by boat, and Margot and I devoured each issue as it arrived. Through it we learned of the ever increasing popularity of ballet back home, of the brilliant partnership of Anton Dolin and Alicia Markova, and of the emergence in 1933 of the so-called 'baby ballerinas' Baronova, Toumanova and Riabouchinska. Margot also took great interest in the all-England dance competitions in which she had been so successful. In the ballet world certainly Shanghai was a long, long way from London . . .

As soon as we found a flat we settled down and made new friends, amongst whom was an English woman called Mrs Brae. It was she and her daughter June who inadvertently pushed us into the next step of Margot's eventual career.

June was absolutely mad about dancing, and Mrs Brae in turn worshipped her daughter. She had found three Russian dancing teachers for June and an American friend to study with. One was a woman who had a studio, the other two were men with no studios. Undaunted, Mrs Brae cleared her sitting room, had a *barre* installed, and she herself played the piano during the lessons.

As soon as I met Mrs Brae and learnt about all of this I asked whether Margot could join in as well. We were very pleased when she readily agreed. The next day we all went to the studio of the woman teacher. After watching I decided that, according to our standards, she was ruining the children by letting them do movements which their muscles were not then ready or strong enough to take. I also noticed that she was letting June turn her legs out from the knee and not from the hip, which was a very serious fault. I told Mrs Brae all of this and said that I would not allow Margot to take the class and advised her to take June out of it as well. Fortunately she was impressed with my knowledge and none of us went there again.

Of the two men one, Gontcharov, was a fully trained Russian emigré from the Bolshoi Theatre in Moscow, so we were very lucky to find him. The other, Elirov, was an older plump man who had never been a dancer himself, although his wife had. He evidently had watched a lot and now taught what he called *plastique* dancing. It was a sort of cross between Isadora Duncan, classical, and any other type of dance he had seen whose movements pleased him. I thought he was doing no harm, if not much good. June loved his class and we were interested in it as well for the exercises he gave were generally graceful and soft, and not likely to strain any muscles. Of the two, however, there was no question that Gontcharov was the better teacher.

June was an exceptionally keen and bright student and her interest in these classes fired Margot's ambition to do even better. Margot never could stand to be number two in anything . . . naturally by then we were all good friends, and the Braes' attitude strongly influenced ours and vice versa. June was two years older than Margot. She was about fourteen at the time and Margot twelve.

After a while Mrs Brae, following June's desire to 'get on', decided that she would take her daughter back to London to study with the famous Nicholas Legat who at one time partnered Pavlova and who was reputed to be an excellent teacher. Margot was by now fourteen and anxious to join them.

This led me to one of the most difficult decisions I ever had to make. My husband's work was in Shanghai, and taking Margot back to London would mean leaving him for an extended period of time, which naturally was upsetting for both of us. We discussed the situation at great length and it was finally agreed that as Margot had progressed as far as she could in Shanghai, the only place to find out if indeed she had a particular talent for dancing was back home. We decided that if Margot and I travelled to London a few months in advance of his next period of home leave it would allow us time to assess her potential before he arrived for a united family holiday.

Once we arrived in London I decided that the Legat classes, which June was attending, were far too advanced for Margot. All the students were in their early teens. Some were good, some not so good, but one thing I didn't like was that the teacher seldom corrected them. I considered this extremely important because if you don't receive correction when you are young things become much more difficult later on.

From studying the dance magazines I decided that the teacher whom we should next go and see was Princess Serafine Astafieva, who had taught our most famous dancers Alicia Markova and Anton Dolin. I found out where she lived and made an appointment. It was a fascinating and historic house in the King's Road, Chelsea and still stands there, isolated, as it awaits a modern building development that is due to surround it on three sides. Its name, The Pheasantry, recalls its origins when Chelsea was a country village.

The interview was initially discouraging, to say the least. There sat Astafieva, huddled next to a stove in a small dark room whose walls were replete with Russian tapestries. She was old, and very obviously ill, and when I asked her if there was any chance of her teaching my daughter, she refused categorically, stating that she didn't want any more students. I persisted, pleading that I had brought my child six thousand miles, all the way from China, to study with her as she had been responsible for Markova and Dolin! 'They don't care, they never come to see me,' she said. It wasn't true, but she was filled with Russian gloom. In the end, however, she gave in. She dismissed us with a curt 'OK, I look. Come tomorrow.'

Margot loved Astafieva from the start. She was an inspired teacher and her lessons full of dance movement as opposed to the rather dry exercises that some teachers make out of ballet.

One of the hallmarks of a great teacher is to be able to see exactly and immediately why a student has difficulty executing certain steps, and to suggest adjustments to the part of the body concerned in order to facilitate the movement. Astafieva was a genius at this, and she made Margot's work much easier for her

I enjoyed the classes, as spectator, every bit as much as Margot, but I realised that with her nearing fifteen it had come to the point where I had to know if all this training was going to lead somewhere; I just couldn't continue to spend all this time, money and effort on my daughter's occupation if it wasn't. The only place I could find out if she had the talent for a theatrical future was a place where that talent might be used – a ballet company.

When I discussed with Astafieva the idea of taking Margot to the Vic-Wells Ballet School, she was indignant at first. Perhaps she couldn't bear the thought of relinquishing another student. Anyway, she finally agreed that perhaps it was the best thing to do. Margot found all this very difficult to accept as she didn't think she was ready, and as she was very happy where she was. However, she took my word for it.

Unaware of what was to happen, we went along to the Sadler's Wells Theatre unarmed with practice clothes or ballet shoes. And so it was that Margot had to audition barefoot and in her petticoat. After ten minutes she was accepted into the school, and soon afterwards it was Ninette de Valois, the Director of the Company, who took charge of her dancing career. I was no longer actively involved and at first I felt frightened, and then let down, but as I said, there comes a point when you have to let them go, and I did.

I shall never forget the excitement when, four weeks later, we received a postcard asking Margot to attend a rehearsal for a corps de ballet role in the 'snowflake' scene of the ballet *Casse-Noisette*. That meant that she was really IN! She had got her toe on the bottom rung of the ladder, and I had made the correct decision after all.

Nowadays, people see me in a theatre and they exclaim, 'How proud you must be of your daughter.' Well, I am very happy with my daughter's success! I am happy that she has been able to give so many people such great pleasure – but my Grandma used to say that 'Pride comes before a fall' – and falls are bad for dancers!

Part Two

When a man has been guilty of a mistake,
either in ordering his own affairs, or in
directing those of State, or in commanding an
army, do we not always say: So and so has
made a false step in this affair? And can making
a false step derive from anything but lack of
skill in dancing?

MOLIÈRE (1622–1673)

12. Types of Dance

Ballet

Ballet is a word which can cause some confusion when talking of dance. It is used in various contexts to mean different things. It originates from *ballo* in Italian and *bal* in French, meaning dance in the sense of 'a dance' or 'a ball'; that is to say a social occasion at which people dance. The Italian word *balleto* was used in the sixteenth century for a series of social dances usually performed by, but not limited to, couples.

In the sixteenth and seventeenth centuries, some of these social occasions became so elaborate that they included entertainments of music, poetry and dance, somewhat like a lavish cabaret at a private party performed by the host and his friends. In France, this entertainment became known as a *Ballet*.

When these entertainments moved from the great halls of royal palaces into real theatres, the dance element was developed and eventually separated from the speech or poetry. It retained the title ballet. So, first of all, ballet means a stage performance of dance. It can be any kind of dance.

When ballet first moved into the professional theatre it began to evolve a system of technique based quite simply on the social dances of the day. These social or ballroom dances were complicated; every respectable young man and woman spent a considerable amount of time perfecting the many difficult steps. For ease and grace it was necessary to turn the feet out towards the side in order to move rapidly with the utmost control.

In the theatre, it was only a question of elaborating these same steps with more intricate footwork, and adding more leaps and jumps and turns. Lo and behold! There was the style or technique of dancing that we now call ballet.

So it is really nothing more than a legitimate development of the minuet and other eighteenth-century social dances. What makes it seem so far removed from everyday life is the footwear. Whereas ballroom, tap, jazz and folk dancing are done in normal shoes or boots, and modern dance is done in bare feet, only ballet dancers and gymnasts wear close-fitting little slippers with soft soles and no heels; and the women's toe shoes could be regarded as almost freakish if one were not accustomed to them.

But as more of the work-a-day wear of dancers and athletes, such as tights, leotards and tracksuits are adapted for casual fashion wear, so ballet becomes less and less remote from everyday life – almost back to where it started!

Another confusion is caused by references to Russian ballet, English ballet, American ballet and so on. It is sometimes hard to know what is meant. People ask me which training is best, but in fact all ballet training is basically the same. There are, however, big differences in detail and choice is a matter of personal taste. English training produces an effect of effortlessness; American training develops speed and agility.

The expression 'Russian ballet method' does not have any precise meaning. Before the Russian Revolution the style of training in Moscow differed from that in St Petersburg – Moscow dancers were more flamboyant; St Petersburg dancers were softer. Soviet Russian training which is different again in style, now accentuates high leaps and strength. Both the Leningrad and Moscow schools have evolved and moved closer to each other but still retain individual characteristics.

In spite of all these variations in detail, the technique is standard and universal. It presents no problems for ballet dancers of one nationality to perform in the ballet company of any other country.

'Classical ballet' is another confusing term. These days it is sometimes used to mean the type of training that we call ballet, and it is also applied to those ballets created in Russia during the late nine-teenth century that are performed, either complete or in excerpts, in versions that are more or less related to their original productions. *Swan Lake*, *The Nutcracker*, *The Sleeping Beauty*, *Don Quixote*, *The Bayadère*, *Paquita*, and *The Corsaire* are the ones seen most frequently outside Russia, and only the first four of those are shown in their entirety. (*Giselle* dates from an earlier period, the 1840s, and is classified as a 'romantic' ballet.)

A Ballet Class

A ballet class is divided into two sections: the first warms up the body and prepares it for the second part which is the practice of sequences of steps. The whole class prepares the dancer to rehearse a ballet and the rehearsal prepares the dancer for a performance. (In a way each performance is a rehearsal for the performance that will follow; but not without starting again at the beginning with class!)

I talk about preparing the body because the material to be trained consists of muscles, tendons, ligaments, joints and so on. These must become so familiar with each movement that they can be said to have learnt them. But they are not selective; they will learn anything they repeat often enough. Without the mind constantly sending instruc-tions, checking and correcting, they will just as likely learn the movements wrongly. It is an annoying fact that the wrong way to do an exercise is initially the easiest way, and muscles, being lazy by nature, look for whatever gives them the least trouble. In the long run this results in more trouble because ballet technique is so scientifically devised that the more correctly it is performed the easier it becomes.

If we start at the performance and look back, the function of the class may be clearer. A dancer on the stage – a very professional one – looks completely at ease, the movements flow one into another apparently without thought and one could easily believe the dancer improvises as the mood takes him. But watch the movement care-fully; he throws one leg forward, rises in the air with the other leg behind him; he lands on the first leg without a jolt (the leg behind still in the air) then goes immediately and smoothly into another movement. That one jump has taken hours and hours of preparation and repetition over several years. In performance the public is hardly aware of the two little steps that have prepared his force for the take-off, nor the arms moving simultaneously in their own directions contributing to the preparatory force. They notice the arm thrust forward at the height of the jump; it is the opposite arm to the leg that is in front, it has helped the dancer to rise off the ground, it helps to propel him forward and, after he has landed it moves in co-ordination with the rest of the body towards the next important effort.

Co-ordination is the key-note. Each arm, each leg, foot, the head and shoulders all have their part to play and the exact moment to play it. It all happens so quickly, like the different musical instruments of an orchestra combining to produce a bar of a symphony, that it would be impossible for the brain to think of so many different things at once. The body has to be trained until everything responds simultaneously to a single impulse from the brain.

The first section of the class concentrates on warming muscles, working tendons to make them supple and loosening joints. It consists of exercises that are basic to the types of movement that compose the second part of the class.

All the exercises are done in the 'turned out' position which is fundamental to every movement in ballet technique. The legs are 'turned out' from the hip joint which means that the knee caps face towards the sides instead of forwards as is normal.

In order to work in this position, without undue strain during the warming up, the dancer holds onto a *barre* (a rail fixed at about elbow-height).

Beginners face the *barre* and hold with both hands, then progress to the normal manner of holding with the left hand while working the right leg, then turning to hold with the right hand while exercising the other leg.

There are five positions of the feet on the floor, but only four of them are the really basic positions: they are 1st, 2nd, 4th and 5th.

(3rd position is half way to 5th and used mainly by beginners until they can achieve 5th.)

Two of the basic positions are 'closed', i.e. the feet touching each other:

    1st position   – side by side with heels touching;
    5th position   – one in front of the other (like sardines in a tin);
    (3rd position – the feet touching from heel to instep only, or half
                way to 5th position.)

The other two are 'open' positions, i.e. the feet are separated:

    2nd position – side by side;
    4th position – one in front of the other.

There are two 4th positions:

    4th open   – in front of 1st position;
    4th crossed   – in front of 5th position.

(If the dancer is not facing squarely to one wall of the room but facing one of the corners the 2nd position is called *ecarté* and the 5th or 4th (or 3rd) positions become 5th or 4th (or 3rd) crossed or open, depending on which foot is in front of the other.)

    Always in one of the basic positions, or a development thereof, the feet, or one foot, can be:

1) On the ground and bearing weight of the body:

    Whole foot on the ground;
    Heel raised;
    On the toe – girls only;
    Toe touching the ground – but bearing no weight.

2) Off the ground:

    Foot fully stretched;
    Ankle flexed.

The dancer's legs are always in one of the four basic positions – or moving to one of those positions – whether:

The weight of the body is on one or both legs;
One or both knees are bent;
One leg is extended and touching the floor, or raised to any height, straight or bent;
One foot is touching the other leg at the – ankle
– mid-calf
– knee;
Both feet are off the floor.

The movement of the legs to any position never displaces the hips and the legs are always turned out. A movement can also be from the knee down, without moving the thigh.

All the foot and leg positions have their appropriate arm positions or choice of arm positions. The movement of arms from one position to another is called *port de bras*; it can be done with or without moving the legs.

Each composite position of feet, legs and arms has its appropriate position, or choice of positions of the torso, either:

erect;
inclined forward from the hips;
inclined sideways, from the waist up;
turned to the side, from the waist up;
arched backwards, from above the waist (shoulder blades);
bent fully forwards, backwards or sideways;
the shoulders alone turned a little to one side (Epaulé).

Each composite position of feet and legs, torso and arms has its appropriate head position, either:

erect;
inclined forward, backwards, or to one side;
turned half-way or completely to one side;
turned and inclined.

Whenever the dancer is not in a composite position, the feet and legs and/or arms and/or torso and/or head are moving in co-ordination with each other to the next position. Even in movement there is always a precise place in which all the components should be at any given moment. To achieve this co-ordination the dancer needs precise control.

Control needs strength; strength is developed by repetition (the French word for a rehearsal is *répétition*).

Muscles and tendons have to be prepared by gentle stages to accept the enormous variety of movements.

All the exercises done at the *barre* are either part, or the whole, of steps which will be done in the centre of the room.

They are exercises for:

1 – Bending the knees with the weight on both legs; and also,
     Bending one knee, the other foot touching the ground without bearing weight, or off the ground.

   Purpose: to make the tendons supple – achilles in particular;
            warm the muscles;
            gently exercise the knee and ankle joints;
            strengthen the thigh muscles.

2 – Extending one leg to any height keeping the weight on the other leg, and also:

   Transferring the weight from one leg to both, or to the other leg – or from both legs to one.

   Purpose: to stretch and relax muscles;
            exercise foot muscles;
            exercise ankle and hip joints;
            strengthen leg muscles, particularly the thigh.

3 – One foot striking against the other ankle or calf.

   Purpose: to exercise and strengthen the ankle and knee joints.

73

4 – Circling one leg on the floor or in the air.

Purpose: to exercise and strengthen the hip and knee;
strengthen the thigh muscles.

5 – Raising heels from the floor with the weight on one or both legs.

Purpose: to strengthen foot muscles.

All these movements are done in an infinite variety of combinations.
The exercises holding onto the *barre* can last between ten and thirty
minutes – or more.

The second section of the class, in the centre of the room, is divided
into different types of movement:

1 – Centre practice: repetition of some or all the *barre* exercises.

2 – Port de bras: arrangement of arm and torso movements, with or
without leg movements.

3 – Adagio: arrangement of different sustained movements mostly
standing on one leg.

4 – Allegro: small quick movements that slide, jump, travel, change
weight, etc.

5 – Pirouettes: all kinds of turns.

6 – Batterie: all kinds of small jumps in which the feet beat across
each other.

7 – Elevation: all kinds of high and travelling jumps or turning
jumps.

8 – *Sur la pointe* (girls): all kinds of steps that:
    rise onto the toes of one or both feet;
    step straight onto the point of one foot;
    hop or jump on the toes (small jumps).

Jumping steps, small or high, can be:

    jumping from both feet, landing on both;
    jumping from both feet, landing on one foot;
    jumping from one foot, landing on both feet;
    jumping from one foot, landing on one.

They can stay on one place, travel, or turn.

Arrangements of steps can include any of the different types of steps mixed together. An arrangement is called an *enchaînement*.

The two sections of class together, *barre* and centre, normally last from forty-five minutes (beginners) to one and a half hours. Children attending class once or twice a week only touch the tip of the iceberg so far as the full range of technique is concerned. The possible combinations and permutations of steps are so infinite that a famous teacher in Russia is said never to have given the same arrangement of steps twice in all his daily classes over many years.

Serious students should have daily classes from the age of twelve – or ten if possible – because it is impossible to cover all the types of movement *thoroughly* in one class or even in three classes a week. Some teachers plan a general class that covers all the types briefly but concentrates particularly on one different type each day of the week. Others have different systems to ensure that students who attend daily work through all the necessary movements each week.

Point practice for girls is best done in an extra fifteen or twenty minutes at the end of class and in some additional classes once or twice a week. It is not, of course, for beginners but for intermediate and advanced students.

Dancing on point is an extension of the normal class work and does not include a different range of steps. It is usual to do the daily class in soft toes or very old point shoes, and then change into usable toe shoes to practise steps selected especially to strengthen the dancer's technique in that area.

There are certain steps that cannot be done on point – obviously the high jumps are impossible because the push-off from toe tip gives a very limited elevation, and landing from any height onto the toe would be akin to an unsuccessful parachute drop. Even if a dancer's knees and feet were physically strong enough to withstand the impact the aesthetic effect would be hideous. Small hops and jumps on the point are perfectly possible and form an important part of advanced technique; pirouettes are enhanced by turning on the point of the foot because it approximates more closely to the base of a spinning top.

If there are boys and girls in class together the girls do point work at the end when the boys do turns in the air (jumping and turning at the same time) which are not part of the girls' repertoire, and extra steps of high elevation; also certain pirouettes used more often by male dancers than female.

A girl's point class is additional to the daily class and concentrates entirely on point dancing as used on the stage. Boys and girls also have to learn partnering. In this, the brunt of the work is taken by the boy, but the girl must learn to help as much as possible by not throwing herself off balance and expecting to be retrieved smoothly, or making it impossible for her partner not to drop her from a lift. These are called pas-de-deux classes and, like all the others, last about one and a half hours. The girls wear toe shoes.

Ballet training has changed quite a lot during this century. It now concentrates on developing the whole body rather than primarily the legs and arms. The old-fashioned training over-worked the legs and developed the calf muscles. Nowadays the training actually improves the dancer's figure.

The well-trained dancer is one who has achieved masterly control over his body and is free to employ it as a truly expressive medium of art.

Modern Dance

Modern dance differs radically from ballet in concept, practice and attitude. As we have seen, ballet is a style of dancing based on a universal and set vocabulary of steps and positions. The ballet dancer, through years of training, learns this vocabulary, and the choreographer uses it in seemingly endless combinations to produce the desired effect.

Modern dance has no such universal vocabulary. It is more natural in concept and its movements are dictated by the individual artist-choreographer to suit his choreographic needs. There is no one, all-encompassing style of modern dance for there are as many styles as there are choreographers. The constant factor in this art does not lie in technique, but rather in motivation. In all modern dance the movement must come from within. The purpose of a modern dance class therefore is to prepare the dancer's body to be receptive to the intensely personal creative urges of the choreographer.

The modern or contemporary dance has its roots in central Europe and America in the early part of this century at a time when ballet dancing in those areas was regarded as meaningless, rigid and dead. In Switzerland and Germany a small group of experimentalists gathered around Rudolf von Laban who studied the relation of movement to religion, science, astrology, medicine, psychology, education and so forth, producing many original theories and inspiring others to innovative dance creation.

At the same time Isadora Duncan, with her efforts to return dance to the ancient Greek ideals of natural beauty, led other American followers to search out fresh sources of inspiration. Almost contemporary with her was Ruth St Denis who was more involved in the ancient mysteries of Egypt, India and the East. She had a superb sense of theatre and took infinite pains to create an appropriate atmosphere for each of her solo oriental dances. Unlike Isadora Duncan, who danced alone or with a background of girls, St Denis chose to work with a young man who shared her idealism and they formed a partnership which led to their marriage. He was called Ted Shawn and it was as a result of his influence that, in 1915, they co-founded the first modern dance company and school in America. They called it Denishawn.

From its inception, the Denishawn company was concerned with production. Duncan had been content to present her art to the European public simply and directly – Ted Shawn was sufficiently sensitive to the taste of the American public to know that it required more elaborate presentation. In that sense, the company was commercial. They relied heavily on ornate costumes, decor and lighting to present their highly stylised interpretations of Egyptian and Indian gods and goddesses. On the other hand, they took dance seriously. They were intent on presenting to the public an art form capable of expressing what St Denis often referred to as 'The most noble thoughts of man'.

Some of the most famous names in contemporary modern dance were launched through the Denishawn company. Among these were Doris Humphrey, Charles Weidman and the most famous modern dancer/choreographer of all, Martha Graham.

The new generation was primarily concerned with getting back to basics. All of them rejected in the end the stylised approach to dance they had been taught. The two world wars played a role in shaping their concepts. It was time for American dance to assert its independence. Out went all the elaborate costumes and productions – in came simple and severe long dresses for women and workmen's shirts and trousers for men. Modern dance, if it was to succeed, needed a radical approach, if necessary at the expense of public popularity. The new choreography reflected the need to express personal experience as it related to current society; it also reflected a new concern for body rhythms.

Martha Graham developed her theory of contraction and release to correspond to the natural body movements of inhaling and exhaling. Doris Humphrey considered all movement to be a matter of equilibrium – of balance and imbalance – and so she developed her theory of 'fall and recovery'.

Graham looked inward. She was concerned with making visible the 'interior landscape'. Her choreography was sharp and angular in the beginning and full of percussive attack. Later it became somewhat modified by more lyrical movement, but what was present then and is still present today is a kind of inner alertness, a stressed tension whereby the dancer always seems poised on the brink of danger and discovery.

She developed and refined her own technique, based on her theory of contraction and release of energy of which a striking feature is the impulse starting at the core of the body, the spine, and flowing out to the ends of the limbs. Her choreography explored and continues to explore all forms of human emotion and awareness. Her works are many layered – full of psychological and symbolic significance. Her themes are many and varied, but she seems to have found a great deal of inspiration in ritual, in American heritage, and in Greek myth which, like Duncan, she felt was the prototype for all human feeling. Throughout her life, she has been committed to the use of new musical scores and starkly modern designs to accompany her works.

Martha Graham is an American genius whose work is respected and performed all over the world. She retired from the performing stage in 1969 at the age of seventy-five, but continues to be an active choreographer, teacher and company director to the school she founded in 1927.

The technique she evolved is certainly the most popular one ever devised for modern dance and it will continue to live and develop in the hands of the myriad dancer/choreographer/teachers who have passed through her company – among the many are Anna Sokolow, Alwin Nikolais, Paul Taylor and Merce Cunningham.

The London Contemporary Dance Theatre was founded on Martha Graham's principles in 1966 and its faculty is comprised of three of her disciples, Robert Cohan, Robert North and Jane Dudley. It is the only professional British dance company of its kind and has achieved an excellent international reputation through its tours of Europe and the United States as well as its extensive tours of Great Britain.

The company itself numbers up to 25 and has its own open school which offers various courses for the professional dancer. Although the technique is firmly based on the Graham style, the faculty have, over the past decade, refined and adapted it to suit the British modern dancer. In addition to the Graham-based technique, all professional

79

students and dancers in the company are required to take a daily classical ballet class. The school is recognised by the Department of Education and Science and is a College of Further Education offering widely based training for the artistic dancer with special opportunities to learn and practise choreography and teaching

Whereas Graham looked inward, to the 'interior landscape' of the human soul, Doris Humphrey looked primarily at the relationship of the individual to outside forces. Her works were broadly heroic in concept and represented more often than not a triumph over adversity. Unlike many modern dancers of her generation, she had a good foundation in ballet training. She also co-choreographed several pieces with Ruth St Denis for the Denishawn company. Perhaps this is why she was not as violent and radical in her attitudes towards the contemporary idiom as Martha Graham.

She left Denishawn in 1928 with Charles Weidman and together they formed a company and school dedicated to developing her technique based on her principle of 'fall and recovery'. She wrote a book about this called *The Art of Making Dances* and it is now respected as one of the great treatises on the subject.

The Humphrey–Weidman school and company built a repertory richly varied in style and theme, but always true to the premise that emotion comes before movement. Humphrey's choreographic talent ranged from simple studies based on nature to choreographically more difficult subjects like *The Shakers*, about an American religious sect, and abstract works danced to the music of Bach and Grieg.

Weidman was a great teacher as well as being a fine choreographer. He had a subtle sense of humour and he tended to provide lighter elements in the repertory, some of them semi-autobiographical and others based on the books of James Thurber.

The Humphrey–Weidman students were encouraged to retain their individualism and so their disciples such as José Limon, Sybil Shearer and Ann Halprin went on to develop unique personal styles, never carbon copies of their mentors.

This short review is by no means comprehensive, but from it we see how modern dance evolved and how different it is from ballet in practice and concept.

There are other technical differences that have not been discussed. Ballet is based on turned-out positions. That is why the ballet dancer, in order to train the muscles, must train while comparatively young. In modern dance the turn-out is not so extreme, and because point work is not used at all it is possible for the prospective dancer to commence training at a later age.

The dancer's relation to the floor or ground is one of modern dance's most important features. Whereas in ballet the dancer is concerned with lightness, elevation and defiance of gravity, the modern dancer uses the ground as a source of stability and strength. The back, which is held firm and strong in ballet, can be rounded and supple in modern dance.

These days the two art-forms have a mutual respect for one another. The younger modern dancers do not feel the same hostility towards ballet as the founding generation did; many actually take ballet training along with their modern classes because they recognise that this kind of formal training adds discipline and strength and makes them more accomplished artists. Also, many essentially modern choreographers work within the ballet idiom, among them Glen Tetley, Alvin Ailey and Twyla Tharp. Likewise, ballet choreographers are increasingly influenced by modern movement.

Although completely different in nature, there is no doubt that ballet and modern dance have had and will continue to have a considerable effect on one another.

A Modern Dance Class

Of all the modern dancers in the world today, Martha Graham has progressed the farthest in establishing a set technique and a method for training the dancer's body. This method is taught in many professional dance schools and is often called 'Contemporary Dance'.

While it is not practicable to describe fully all the exercises used in a Graham class, it is possible to discuss the theory behind the technical training she advocates. She believes that all exercises should be based on the structure of the body, and that all of them should be extensions of its inherent physical capabilities. As such, there should be no artificial or forced movements. She also believes that as dance is motion, all exercises should be based on the body in motion as its natural state. She believes that training has three purposes, to strengthen, to liberate, and to prepare the body and soul to accept spontaneity of action.

All exercises in a Graham class are in the form of theme and variation. The exercise starts with a specific area simplified of all extraneous movement or embellishment, and then widens in scope to incorporate the use of the entire body.

The Graham class is divided into four main categories: floor exercises, exercises standing in one place, elevation exercises, and finally exercises for falls.

The floor exercises comprise leg extensions, stretching and back exercise. They incorporate her theory of contraction and release to correspond with the natural body rhythm of inhaling and exhaling. There should be no forcing of any movement in these exercises. Strength must be allowed to develop slowly and gradually. These exercises are meant to prepare the body for the following standing and elevation sections.

The second section involves all exercises for the legs, hips, feet, and finally turns in place. In all *pliés*, the moderate turned out position is used. As with ballet, in all *plié* work, close attention is paid to the knees and feet. The movement must come from the hip. The knees must not be allowed to roll inward.

The next section involves all exercises for elevation. These include leaps, skips, turns in the air, runs and jumping in place. All previous exercise should have strengthened the body sufficiently to perform these without strain.

The final section concerns fall and recovery. The dancer learns to fall from various positions using different rhythms. The whole process should be a means of affirmation. The body never remains on the floor, but rises to an upright position as part of the exercise. The motivation must come from within, and on no account must the spine or the knees strike the floor. The energy must be contained in the legs and the arms.

Graham believes that her classes should not only be intended for professional use. She believes that they can be of serious emotional and physical benefit to both the untrained adult and to the child.

Stage Dance

This term applies to dance in the so-called lighter forms of theatrical entertainment such as musicals, revues, cabaret, and any associated presentations of that nature. The types of dancing called for in these entertainments can be just about anything and everything that the dancers can do. They are also expected to sing. Training includes tap dancing and jazz, some modern dance and ballet.

The big difference between working in this medium or specialising in ballet or modern dance is that whereas the dance companies present a changing repertoire with the same group of performers, stage dancers are engaged for the run of one particular show. The variety of roles in a changing repertoire allows for a slow but continuous artistic development. The dancer in a show must repeat the same performance endlessly with unflagging energy and enthusiasm, which requires extraordinary discipline but does not reward him with a sense of progress.

A Jazz Class

The purpose of a jazz class is to introduce a supple strength into the body coupled with a strong sense of rhythmic co-ordination. It is aimed at the professional dancer who works in the musical theatre, film and television business. However, it has become increasingly popular with the non-professional because it is such a pleasant and enjoyable way of toning and firming the body, as well as keeping fit in general.

There are many different types of jazz class: modern, rock and soul being a few examples. As with modern dance, the technique that is taught depends on the teacher. As there is no *barre* work and only a limited use of the turned out positions, most professional dancers supplement their jazz training with ballet classes.

A typical jazz class is divided into four sections: stationary isolation exercises; floor exercises; jumps, turns and balancing exercises; final combination.

The purpose of isolation exercises is to train the dancer to be able to use each part of his body independently. The dancer faces front, feet parallel, about eighteen inches apart. In this section, he works on the head, the neck, the shoulders, the ribcage, the hips, and the legs and feet.

Each part of the body from the head to the hips is exercised in two ways: first the slow continuous roll front, right, back, left, followed by the more static right, centre; left, centre; front, centre; back, centre. Then comes a series of slow *pliés*, demi and full, in comfortable modified first and second positions.

The purpose of floor exercises is to work on the extension of the legs, control of the back, and strengthening of the abdominal muscles. The dancer sits on the floor with the soles of his feet placed together. He holds his ankles with his hands and bounces forward, first with a straight back and then with a curved one so that his head almost touches his feet. Then he combines these two movements into one continuous flowing action. Then he extends his legs, feet pointing outward (this is sometimes called sitting in second position) and goes through a series of pointing and flexing of the legs and feet. This is followed by a series of sit-ups, and other exercises designed to tighten the abdominal muscles.

These two sections comprise the warm up part of the class. No further complex movement should ever be attempted before all these exercises have been successfully completed. Otherwise, the dancer risks serious damage to his muscles.

The next series of exercises concerns elevation and turns. In all types of jumping, the force must come from the whole leg and not just the ankle. The movement must first start with a *demi-plié*. In

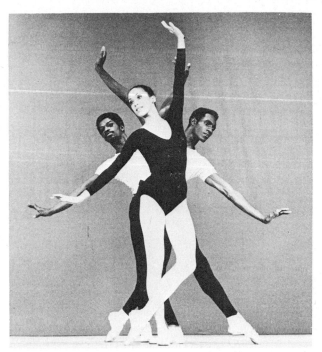

turning, the dancer must learn to spot – that is to focus on an individual point in space – in order to avoid dizziness.

The final section is generally a jazz routine improvised by the teacher, varying in degrees of difficulty and utilising the various exercises taught in class. Sometimes, the routine is built on from class to class.

Jazz classes are available in the beginner, intermediate and advanced levels and last anything from one hour to one and a half hours.

Ethnic Dance

Originally ethnic or folk dances were the traditional dances of each country and each region, in some cases of each village, throughout the world. They were handed down from one generation to the next for centuries, evolving a little on the way but basically unchanged.

Children simply picked them up by copying their elders. They learnt the dances in the same way that they learnt to talk and had no need of teachers.

The pattern of modern life in big cities breaks up that natural cycle and a conscious effort has to be made by ethnic groups to preserve their cultural traditions. This happens most frequently when immigrants in a new country feel the need to maintain the memory and customs of their homeland; but generally speaking the natural folk dance is rapidly dying out.

Luckily dance conservationists seek out and record what has not yet been lost altogether and many folk dance societies are formed to encourage the continuation of old traditions.

National Dance

In the nineteenth century, ballet introduced national dances to add variety to a long evening of otherwise pure ballet dancing. The Polish mazurka and cracovienne, the Hungarian czardas, various Spanish and Italian and Russian dances turned up frequently, using traditional steps and formations rearranged for the stage. (The dances of more distant lands were not known in detail so the wildest imagination went into the creation of Turkish, Scotch or Chinese scenes.)

Once ballet had shown how well folk art adapted to the stage it was an easy step to engage whole troops of dancers in lively and colourful presentations of the national dance heritage. In this century such dance companies are regarded as contributors to international understanding because music and dance, like painting, have no language barrier.

The timeless dances of remote villages which were once accessible only to intrepid travellers now come to those who sit comfortably in the cushioned theatre seats of their home cities; or we can see Mexican, Balinese, African, Korean and many other dance groups at home on our television screens.

Spanish and Indian Dance

Obviously Spanish dancing is ethnic. I only mention it separately because there is such a variety and richness in the dances of Spain, both classical and flamenco, that they are a study in themselves. The same is true of Indian dance which is the most ancient tradition of all and includes several different styles or schools. Remote as the two countries may seem there is, in fact, a very distant relationship between Indian dance and that of the Spanish gypsies.

Spanish training naturally includes the playing of castanets, the exact origin of which would be hard to determine for sure. The use of little wooden clappers was common for dancers in Egypt under the pharaohs, in ancient Greece and in the Middle East as a whole. Turkish and other oriental dancers also used tiny cymbals on thumb and finger to emphasise rhythm and add a charming accent to the musical accompaniment.

Spanish flamenco is the dance of gypsies who travelled from the east through Europe via North Africa to Spain where they settled in the caves around Granada. Their concentration on stamping and foot-work bears witness to their dance's long lost origins in India where the feet make their own soft rhythm as they shake their anklets of tiny bells. Spanish classical dancing is restrained in style as it was the social dance of noblemen and courtiers in earlier times.

Feminity and grace are natural to Indian women and it is a pity that the study of their dance is not more available in the occident for it would be very rewarding. At the moment its study almost requires travelling to India itself. Very few dancers have opened schools in the West and we have too little knowledge of the art and its significance. Perhaps the religious foundations, being so alien to us, have made it a study for the specialists rather than the general public. Many Indian dances are like long narrative ballets depicting sagas of the gods.

Perhaps one day Japanese and Chinese classical dance will also be taught in the West. What better way to understand more of an alien people than to participate in their culture and arts?

Social Dance

Social dancing is ballroom dancing, but since it is as frequently per-formed on a tiny area of floor in a cramped disco, club or nightclub as in the traditional spacious ballroom, 'social' seems a more appro-priate name for this style of dancing. It is a hybrid. It is neither an artificial theatre art like ballet nor is it a completely natural form like ethnic or folk dance.

Social dance originates one way or another in folk dance, but is adapted for completely different circumstances. It is really a commo-dity like fashion, which is affected by social and political conditions and provides a livelihood for those engaged in its trade. The history of social dance is a fascinating and somewhat neglected study.

Social dance is within the reach of everyone and, for those who want to become very involved, there are championship competitions. In Europe the amateur ballroom dancing competitions are very distinguished. They are extremely well organised and pleasing to participants and spectators alike. The Brazilian samba schools provide somewhat of a parallel in the degree of time and hard work that goes to the making of a good team of amateur dancers.

There is a great importance in amateur dancing whether com-petitive or not. It is a contact with the fundamental and natural roots of our existence. People who live in big cities are deprived, con-sciously or unconsciously, of those almost indefinable things on which our human sensitivity feeds, like the first breath of morning country air imperceptibly scented by dew; the glint of late afternoon sun through pale green leaves; the whiff of wood smoke or even the distant sound of barking carried across fields. A million little bonuses of nature are denied the city dweller, his subconscious is under-nourished and his need for art is greater than that of country folk.

Some people's senses are deprived and they need the visual and auditory arts: others are deprived physically, the journey to work by underground is no substitute for a brisk country walk. The physical and emotional enjoyment of dancing, unrelated to the responsibilities of stage performance, is one way of compensating for some of the stresses caused by concrete jungle living.

13. The Student

A student of dance is a person working seriously to make a career in the art. As a profession, dance has its hazards like any other art. Nevertheless I believe it to be the best and most agreeable life because people who perform on the stage enjoy some sort of special magic not really found anywhere else.

No-one should go into the theatre who is not suited to the way of life. Regular hours and free week-ends are unknown. None of the arts can be regarded purely as a job to be carried out within pre-ordained hours. It is necessary to have some sense of perfection and the will to do whatever is required to give of one's best. This is something that dancers in general do have and it is one of the things that makes dance an agreeable career, because it is satisfying to work with people one respects. Whether the work is hard or not is difficult to say, and anyway what does it matter so long as it is enjoyable?

I am always surprised by the number of people who ask what dancers do to keep fit for the strenuous life they lead. The answer is, of course, just the reverse – it is the strenuous life that keeps them fit. Students do make efforts these days to be slim, and probably watch their diets, but I cannot believe it right to take so much exercise without sufficient protein and such other nutrients as the body needs – which may differ with each individual. To project a performance to the public takes energy and enthusiasm, two things which don't come easily to the under-nourished. It is not sufficient on stage to go through steps and movements as in a classroom, the same steps become something quite different when they are used to express the theme and character of the choreography; they must be transformed

93

and given to the public as a 'performance' and carry with them that magic that is the secret of the theatre. No one can say exactly what makes one performer stand out from all the others and catch the attention of every member of the public. It is not only a case of dancing better than the others but also of deep concentration, and involvement in the meaning of what is danced.

Of necessity, students must work to the utmost to perfect their control and strength of movement, but over and above that aspect they must not overlook what dancing is all about. The classroom is never more than a preparation for the stage and that is where judgement is made.

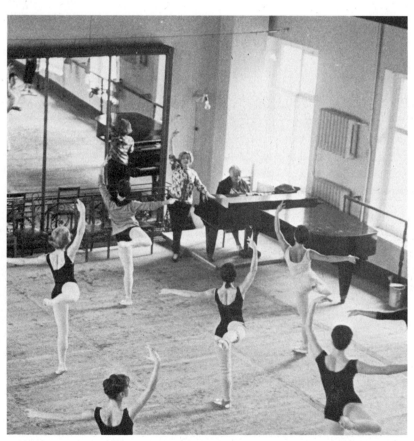

It may be that some students will go instead into other branches of dancing, such as teaching or notation, but that does not alter what I have said. A teacher who has not herself been a professional dancer must still regard the classroom as only a preparation for the stage. For why else do we learn to dance if not to give beauty and pleasure to others? Admittedly, it is a vanity to try to attract the attention of the public to ourselves, but it is not as easy as it seems. The stage demands full value and the public won't look at those who offer a perfunctory performance. Nothing less than our best means putting our hearts and souls into what we are doing.

14. The Dancer

Professional dancers, like other human beings, come in all shapes and sizes but there are certain requisites, both physical and mental, which are important if one is to succeed in this unpredictable profession.

Most schools attached to particular ballet companies insist on an orthopaedic examination of the prospective student before he or she is accepted. Good health, a strong constitution, and a well proportioned body are necessary. Height also is an important consideration, especially for girls, because point shoes add at least six inches. Ideally girls should be between 5ft 2in and 5ft 6in, and although there is really no fixed height for boys, they should in general be between 5ft 7in and 6ft. Of course there are exceptions to this rule, in fact at times nature perversely provides a surfeit of tall ballerinas at the same time as a glut of short male dancers. Generally speaking, the long-legged dancers excel in slow, graceful movements, while the little dancers dazzle with their speed.

It is difficult to predict with certainty the eventual height of a twelve-year-old, but bone measurements and the height of the parents provide quite substantial clues.

Apart from these purely physical qualities, ideally a dancer should be determined, receptive, patient and possess a strong sense of self-awareness. He or she must be able to accept criticism readily for this is a common element in a dancer's life. Above all, and it may seem obvious to state this, a dancer should love to dance.

Every day presents new challenges, new setbacks and a subconscious feeling that all the effort and struggle may not be worth it in the end. Without sheer determination, a dancer is handicapped. The will to succeed in the face of such adversity must be very strong indeed if the dancer is to overcome such inevitable feelings of frustration.

A dancer must be receptive. He or she must be quick to grasp new ideas and the impressions of others. Almost everything in ballet is a collaboration of one sort or other – collaboration between student and teacher, between partners, with the conductor, and especially with the choreographer. Choreography is, more often than not, a collaboration between creator and executor.

Patience is a virtue, especially in dance. Every little girl wants to be able to dance on point from her very first lesson, and I am certain that boys feel the same way about *double tours* and *grand jetés*. But these feats take years of training. Even the accomplished dancer will find some movements completely alien to her, and she must work methodically and conscientiously to perfect them.

Most of a dancer's working life is spent in a classroom in front of a mirror. In this way she becomes aware of her own body and learns to make it move in the way she wants. This brings an extraordinary satisfaction. The dancer comes to know her own limitations and strengths.

A strong personality is a definite asset, for this projects across the footlights as readily and as surely as the most brilliant technique, and can conceal to a certain extent the physical limitations which every dancer has to one degree or another.

Technique, the basis of the art, is, of course, essential and is developed over years of training and hours and hours of bending, stretching and extending various muscles. The artist with a virtuoso technique is truly blessed. In the end, however, it is how one uses that technique that separates the dancer from the athlete. Which brings us to the rather harder qualities to define – qualities such as grace, line, musicality and dramatic ability.

Of these, grace and line are synonymous. A ballet is really a series of linked positions, gestures and movements. Good line, as in sculpture, occurs when it seems that one could draw an unbroken line from the head, through the arms, upper body, down to the feet. It is easy to see how a jutting arm, a leg too highly extended, or a head placed too far forward in certain jumps can destroy the line, as well as the inherent grace. All movements in ballet must seem to flow harmoniously and any awkward or jarring element shatters the effect.

Good line starts with a perfect turn out of the feet, a straight back and proper placing of the head and arms. The dancer who is born with a well-proportioned body, with a slightly elongated neck, with beautiful arms and straight legs is at a distinct advantage compared to others less fortunate. Proper training and a critical eye can do much to improve line, and improper training can destroy it for ever.

It would be wonderful if all dancers were musical – unfortunately they are not. It is largely a matter of instinct. A child is either born with a love of or an ear for music or not. Parents can do much to instil a love of music in their children. It is axiomatic that a child who grows up listening to classical music will find it easier to relate to in later life. Learning to play an instrument like the piano is also beneficial for a child is then actively participating in music. The child will understand something about what music is; that like dancing, it is hard to perform well. Such a child will never again be passive in relation to music.

When creating a new ballet, the choreographer takes his inspiration from the music he has chosen, and so it should be with the dancer. A 'musical' dancer is one who understands and feels the shape and the shadings of the score. He does not merely keep time with it, he relates to it. Naturally when learning a ballet, the dancer must be content for the moment with learning new steps and counting in time to make sure of entrances, exits and placing. Then he must listen harder to the score to learn the phrasing of it, rather like a singer. But once all of this is learnt by rote and becomes automatic, the musical dancer listens, feels and interprets. The music ceases merely to accompany; it dictates, it becomes the inspiration for his every movement.

Dance is one of the performing arts, and a performing artist is, more often than not, an actor at heart. In many ways dance is drama distilled, because the whole range of human emotion must be expressed completely through the body. The dancer has no words to help. The function of ballet, or modern dance, is to tell a story or to express a point of view; to relay a mood or a feeling. It stands to reason that dramatic ability is very nearly as important to the dancer as the ability to negotiate difficult steps.

Some dancers are born with this natural dramatic ability. For others, it comes with experience. It follows that once one has performed a role several times, one can relax into it and concentrate more on its dramatic presentation; to some extent the drama develops itself in the course of performances.

Throughout my life, I have always preferred the dramatic roles because I find the pure steps rather difficult and frightening. If I have a character to immerse myself in, I can think, for instance, about what Giselle is feeling and suffering and forget that the steps are difficult. If I am faced with a ballet which has no story at all and is really just a series of ballet steps, I am over-conscious of the least fault in their execution and I find this inhibiting from the point of view of communicating dance to the public.

Finally, the most important quality a dancer can possess is also the one that is hardest to define. Talent for dancing is something that one is born with. Once it is discovered it can be developed, it can be nurtured – but it can never ever be manufactured.

Curiously, although talent can be discerned in the young one can never be sure how far it will develop. There is also the question of physique which complicates the issue. One looks first for the well-proportioned body, straight legs, suitable foot and strong spine; with the ideal physique one can make an exceptional dancer – but one cannot add the 'divine spark' of expression, emotion or whatever it is that makes a rare artist.

On the other hand, the 'divine spark' often turns up in a less than ideal physique. If it appears in a hopelessly proportioned body there is nothing to be done because the greatest violinist in the world cannot draw magic from an out of tune fiddle and the dancer's body is equivalent to his musical instrument. He depends upon it entirely to transmit his talent to the world.

Between the extremes of a perfect figure with no soul and a genius in the wrong shaped body there are so many permutations that it is quite impossible to say what will make a good dancer and what will not. One must always remember that each one of us is an individual and cannot be ordered over the telephone like a Ford Cortina.

15. A Ballet Company

Ballet is more than a profession – it is a way of life. A ballet company is simply a microcosm of that way of life. When a dancer is accepted, he or she joins an élite family of dedicated people all working towards the same goal with the same purpose. Companies vary considerably in size and scope, ranging from the handful of large and famous institutions like the Royal Ballet and American Ballet Theatre and New York City Ballet to the smaller regional ones like the Scottish National Ballet and the Sacramento Civic Ballet.

Although it may be a dancer's dream to join a famous company, the importance of the smaller regional ones cannot be over-stressed. These companies give dancers and choreographers the chance to develop at their own pace; they have the opportunity for experimentation without overexposure. Also, because of their smaller size, the dancer, especially at the beginning of a career, is given more work and more challenging roles than would be the case if he or she had joined a larger company.

When I joined the Vic-Wells Company in 1933 there were only thirty-six dancers – perhaps only the director, Ninette de Valois, foresaw that it would grow into the Royal Ballet with a company nearing two hundred!

A dancer is accepted into a company in one of several ways. Very occasionally, in the case of a professional with previous stage experience, he or she may be invited to join on the basis of exceptional talent. The two more common ways are either through audition, or by graduating successfully from the school attached to the company – or attached to another important company.

This latter method obviously has the most advantages. Ideally all ballet companies should have their own schools because students are trained from an early age to meet specific requirements. They grow up attending performances of the parent company, watching and learning from its dancers so that by the time they graduate, even before they ever set foot on stage, they have a real idea and knowledge of the company's style and artistic demands.

The Royal Ballet School is divided into two parts. A student can either attend the lower school at White Lodge in Richmond Park where from the age of eleven or twelve he or she is given a comprehensive education along with the dance training, or he or she can attend a regional school and then audition for a place in the upper school at around the age of sixteen. The Royal Ballet and similar companies with such schools accept most of their dancers in this way.

Of course, attending this type of school does not automatically guarantee a place in the company. Students are watched very carefully, and are reassessed every year. Of the relatively few that complete their training successfully, a handful are invited to join the parent company, the rest are advised to attend auditions for other companies. It is a fact that students graduating from a school of this nature have a better than average chance of finding work. Tuition fees are invariably high, but there are government grants and scholarships available in certain circumstances.

When a student is finally accepted into a ballet company, there is an overwhelming sense of relief, of joy and of accomplishment. At last he or she is a professional dancer with a certain amount of emotional, artistic and financial security.

All ballet companies are structured along similar lines. Usually they are divided into four main categories: corps de ballet, coryphées, soloists and principals. The fledgling dancer, except on rare occasions, starts his or her professional life in the corps, the importance of which cannot be overemphasised. Its function is to set the mood of the ballet, to lend depth, continuity and presence to the whole. The emphasis here is placed on precision and togetherness and it is certainly true that a well trained and rehearsed corps can literally make a company's reputation. Dancing in the corps, the individual gains valuable stage experience. From sheer repetition of movement, the brain is disciplined, the body is strengthened, various difficulties are worked out, and personality is developed. Of course the type of corps work varies from ballet to ballet. Some of it is extremely difficult, challenging and hence rewarding for the dancers; and occasionally it might be dull.

The term coryphée is used in many cases to designate a kind of half-way house between corps and soloist. Here the dancers who show promise and individuality are tried and tested in a variety of soloist roles along with maintaining their corps work. If they are successful they will be offered a soloist contract. A soloist theoretically is no longer concerned with corps work. He or she concentrates completely on solo variations, pas de deux, and the occasional principal role. It is with the soloist contract that the dancer begins to dream of stardom and the final accolade, a principal contract! That is the last moment at which anyone should feel complacent. The higher a dancer rises in the company the greater is their responsibility to justify expectations, and the critics do not always appreciate what it means to hold the stage alone in an important role for the first time.

The length of time spent in each of these particular categories is strictly dependent on the individual's talent and ability. It is a sober fact of ballet life that the majority of dancers never progress beyond the coryphée stage. The world, fortunately, is made up of different people with different temperaments. Some are ambitious, some are not. There must come a point in a coryphée's life where a certain amount of stock-taking is necessary. Some know they will never progress beyond this point and face the fact with equanimity. They remain in the company because it has become their way of life and they are happy in the atmosphere of communal artistic enterprise – for one never really loses the sheer love of dancing. Some others ultimately decide it is not the life they really want and they find work in television, films or the musical theatre – or they may leave the world of dance altogether for marriage and children.

A typical day in a dancer's life begins every morning with class. This usually lasts for one and a half hours, although on matinee days there may only be time for *barre* work without the centre practice.

This is the most vital part of a dancer's life, a part that can never be ignored because a dancer's body is like a delicate instrument that constantly needs fine tuning to keep it in performing condition. The older a dancer becomes, the more important it is to take a daily class because, even after a week's holiday, the muscles stiffen and do not respond.

In class everyone from the corps to the principal dancer is subject to criticism and correction. After class there are either full company calls for various new ballets, or more personal ones for dancers either about to perform a role for the first time, or with different partners, etc. New roles are the stuff of life for a dancer, and when such plums are landed it is a sure thing that every spare moment will be spent perfecting them.

'Lunch' (often just an apple and cheese and a yoghurt) is usually taken in the staff canteen or at the café round the corner, and this is followed by more rehearsals, traditionally from 2.00 pm to 4.00 pm,

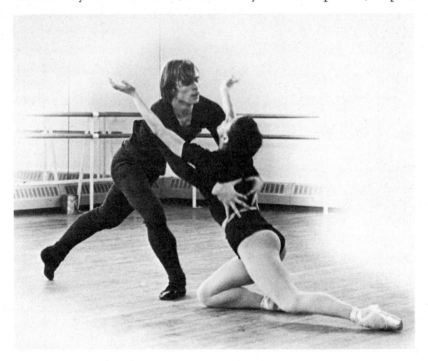

or perhaps by costume fittings. Also, most ballet companies have some kind of workshop whereby fledgling dancer/choreographers can work with members of the company to present their new works on special evenings before an invited audience. In this way even corps de ballet members get involved learning solo roles and they are usually given afternoon rehearsal time. And it must be said that on the odd and blissful occasion a dancer will find himself with a completely free afternoon!

On performance evenings everyone concerned must be at the theatre well in advance because costume, make-up and warming up take a good hour at least; personally, I always allow two hours. These activities can be quite therapeutic. Dancers are always keyed up before a performance. Some are more nervous than others, and the concentration involved in making up, for example, often has a calming effect.

For the next two and a half hours everything must go like clock-work. Dancers leave their real identities in the dressing room and become the characters they are portraying on the stage. The nerves that were present before seem to disappear on stage because the dancer who is physically and mentally involved in the act of perform-ing simply does not have the time to be nervous.

It is after the curtain comes down that a dancer's private life begins. It takes time to wind down after a performance, and although it is late, most dancers take this time to relax with friends over their main meal of the day – because few dancers like to eat much before the performance, although there are some who can sit down to a good steak and then go straight into the theatre for the show.

It is often said that ballet is a closed world, and in a way it is true. It is very difficult to make friends outside the company because of the hours involved and the dedication required. It is difficult, but not impossible. A ballet dancer's life is certainly not easy and it might be prone to more disappointments than any other, yet the people who have chosen to pursue this way of life are for the most part happy, dedicated and fulfilled, because they work continuously with a com-patible group pursuing the same objectives and sharing their sorrows and triumphs.

16. Teachers' Training

The first message of this book is that dancing is for everyone, or at least that it holds something for everyone who wants to involve themselves in it, and that professional ballet is only a part of the whole, although it tends to catch most of the limelight.

The second message is that anyone wanting to study dance, and in this case ballet in particular, should make every effort to be sure they have good teachers.

It may seem strange that in most countries there is no formal registration of dance teachers, and it is for this reason that various organisations have been established during the last fifty years or so to guide teachers on what to teach and how to go about it.

More recently three-year training courses for dance teachers have been set up in one or two cities in England and Canada. Entry to these courses requires a certain level of practical accomplishment in ballet, and the curricula cover anatomy, principles of education, dance history and various subjects equally important for young teachers in this age of unprecedentedly high standards at the corps de ballet level of all dance companies.

As more is expected of the corp de ballet dancers it follows that more is expected of teachers at all levels, especially those who start young children on their very first steps; so much depends on the initial placing of the body, and of the hip joints and the ankles and feet. It is very necessary for teachers to comprehend clearly the mechanics of ballet technique and its application to the various shapes and sizes of human form.

Graduates from the training courses are in immediate demand;

often they have the opportunity to travel and take their first professional jobs with dancing academies far from their home countries. The prospects are good and the work interesting. More information can be found in the dance magazines.

17. Dance as a Subject

Many students these days do not have the means or the physical structure to become professional dancers and yet their intense love of the art seeks fulfilment in a career somehow involved with dance. If they have not taken any dance classes at all it is difficult to take the subject at school or university as a qualification for entry involves some basic level of practical experience.

There are related studies which could lead to the world of dance, the first that comes to mind is stage management which is of the greatest importance and can indeed make or mar a performance. Production has many departments including scene-painting, construction, the making of costumes and props – small items used or carried in performance. Perhaps the most difficult to achieve well is stage lighting as it requires very special knowledge and imagination, also, I would say, a certain flair.

For the students who have taken dance to a certain elementary level there are school and college courses leading towards various basically amateur activities as well as careers in dance history, writing and lectures, notation and anthropology. There are still areas of dance study that have been very little explored.

In England it would be advisable to take the GCE 'O' Level in Ballet and/or the CSE and CEE in Modern Educational Dance. (CSE is more or less the equivalent of an 'O' Level and CEE, the Certificate of Extended Education, the equivalent of an 'A' Level.)

These courses, while in no way preparing teenagers for a career on the stage, do help to provide them with a wider working knowledge of the subject. Along with elementary classes in ballet and modern dance they learn the history of dance and the principles of dance movement. In addition to a final examination, the candidates must write a thesis on the history of dance. They also give a graduation performance.

Recently, a project has developed called the London Youth Dance Theatre. This is comprised of a group of graduates from these courses who give local performances around London. They have also appeared on television.

In the United States, where there is an incredible resurgence of interest in dance, there is no exact parallel to the British GCE, CSE and CEE certificates in dance, but it is possible to obtain a BA or even a Masters Degree in the subject as part of a university education.

18. Choreology

A new career in the world of dance has opened up quite recently – that of choreologist. Choreology is defined as 'the scientific and aesthetic study through notation of all forms of human movement'. It is a science that is still in its infancy. It has taken over five hundred years to perfect an orchestral score. It is fascinating to learn that although a successful system for writing down dance steps was published as early as the eighteenth century by a Frenchman, Raoul Feuillet, it was intended for social dance and therefore limited in its application. The perfected dance notation has only come into its own during the last fifty years.

There are two major notation systems in practice today. One is called Labanotation and was developed from a basis of Feuillet's work by the Hungarian Rudolf von Laban in 1928. The other was invented and copyrighted in 1955 by the English couple Rudolf and Joan Benesh and is called simply the Benesh system. One can study these two systems all over the world. Scores for various ballets are printed and can be bought and read like music.

Simply put, graduates of these two systems work extensively with the choreographer in the dance studio where a ballet or modern work is created. As each movement is set, the choreologist writes it down, and when the work is completed, the notated score is kept as a permanent record and can be sent anywhere in the world so it can be reproduced by other ballet companies. What once was confined to the choreographer's and dancer's memories is now recorded in minute detail in a manuscript, just as music is at the fingertips of anyone who can read a score.

Benesh Notation

Posé in ara-
besque, fondu
with retiré

Relevé
passé
devant

Jeté in atti-
tude front
and back

Développé grand
rond de jambe
to attitude

Labanotation

Labanotation is based on a three line vertical staff, the centre line representing the spine. It uses symbols and shadings to record the type and depth of movement, and has been used in America for many years. It is the system used to record many Broadway shows as well as classical and modern works. All Balanchine ballets have been

Labanotated as well as the works of modern dancers like Doris Humphrey and Martha Graham. When Humphrey's *The Shakers* was revived for the Welsh Dance Theatre in 1975, the company used the Labanotation record of the original choreography.

The Benesh system is based on a five line musical stave and is said to be easier to learn. It is a purely visual system, and the Royal Ballet uses it exclusively. The ballets of Ashton, MacMillan, De Valois and Cranko are mounted all over the world with the aid of Benesh scores.

Naturally, in order to study and practise choreology, one has to have had a certain amount of professional dance training. It goes without saying that without an extensive knowledge of the steps, it is impossible to write them down. The notation training is far from easy, requiring considerable patience and intelligence. It is, however, a fascinating and valuable study.

But the uses of choreology are not limited to dance. The medical profession has become increasingly interested in its application in conjunction with physiotherapy and with recording the movements of pre- and post-operative patients. Consequently, the Institute of Choreology has started giving introductory courses to registered physiotherapists.

Both forms of notation have also been used with a great deal of success in the field of dance anthropology – and what better way to study the nature of man than through his dances? For expressive movement is as old as time itself.

Field anthropologists, in studying human behaviour had no system to record movement and consequently many primitive and tribal dances were lost to human memory.

Roderyk Lange, in his book, *The Nature of Dance* said about Labanotation, 'After many attempts made over the centuries, it has become possible for the first time to put observations of human move-ment into the form of a rational statement, as well as to make a per-manent record of the results in graphic scripts. In this way each and every movement could be comparatively analysed so providing the basis for a scientific approach to movement and dance research.'

Rudolf von Laban, as well as developing a system of dance notation also advanced a theory of movement. He analysed the properties of

human movement and found that one could not divorce physical movement from psychophysical entity. That is, it is not enough to study sheer motion without understanding the inner attitudes that govern it.

This is where Laban's system of notation is so useful. It can record the 'going with' and 'going against' attitudes towards motion factors. The ability to define the 'effort' in movement terms is essential in order to describe specific ways of movement interpretation. With this modern scientific technique field anthropologists can study tribal dances and learn much about the development of man in the process.

19. Movement Expression

Movement expression is not exactly dance but very closely related, and an attractive alternative for those who are not ambitious for dancing careers but are attracted to a very personal exploration of the possibilities of expression without the use of spoken language. Contrarily, it is also an invaluable study for actors, singers and public speakers to help them augment the communicative power of their words.

Movement Expression, also called Body Movement or *L'Expression Corporelle* – they are basically one and the same thing – is simply another means by which the human being can express, and be open to, his innermost feelings and the feelings of others. We practise 'movement' every day of our lives, at all times and under all circumstances. However, to discover and learn about the systems which are activated in movement, for the most part unconsciously, and which help us to communicate with other human beings, we must be able to identify and analyse our emotions.

Whereas ballet teaches a given technique, 'movement' teaches a pupil to discover how the body moves, breathes, relaxes, contracts and reacts to different situations or environments; also the why and wherefore of all conscious and unconscious movement. It is rather like the 'discovery' of oneself – of one's limitations and possibilities – and what one can do to improve. This, of course, will give more self-assurance and more self-awareness through increased perception.

Children crawl, walk, skip, jump, leap, dance and suchlike to their hearts' content until, with the approach of adolescence, they become unsure, inhibited and generally self-conscious about the development of their bodies. Taking 'inventory' of themselves, and learning how to use movement in a natural, unself-conscious manner helps to give them back some badly needed assurance, or, in other words, to improve their 'self-image'.

All movement, whether voluntary or involuntary, conscious or unconscious, comes from the inner self and from the psychosomatic complex which makes up the individual's personality. It cannot avoid expressing the inner emotional state accurately. On the other hand awareness and control of body movement, by the very assurance and fluency they bring to the ordinary motions of walking, standing, sitting and so on, relax some of the inner tensions which are the cause of awkward movement in the first place.

Obviously, when considering all the arts, it is easy to understand how a thorough knowledge of movement expression applied to drama, singing, painting or sculpture could bring tremendous enrichment to their performance; and the classical ideal of harmony and balance in the arts is equally applicable to ordinary life where greater understanding of these forces leads to greater fulfilment.

Classes in movement expression depend very much on the individual teacher who programmes the work to suit the pupils' needs; the subjects taught come under the following general headings, but are intriguingly open to expansion and experimentation. (They do not properly include psychodrama, or role playing, which is imitative, whereas movement expression is creative.)

SENSIBILITY

  the body
  the spine
  the articulations
  tension and relaxation
  respiration (breathing).

SPACE

Space and its importance at all times (personal, partial and total)
  locomotion
  quality of movement
  form (shape)
  effort; energy
  movement with objects.

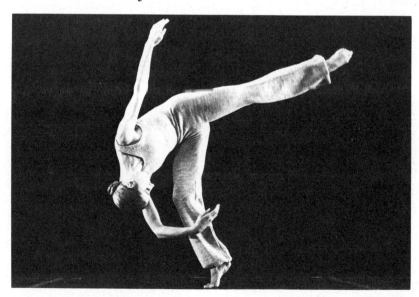

RHYTHM

1) *The body as instrument*
   percussive; stamping, clapping
   flow of movement.

2) *Outside stimulus*
   music
   unrelated sound.

IMPROVISATION

1) *Structured*
   following indications set by teacher

2) *Free*
   the pupil chooses theme, character or situation and the
   movements to be employed in interpretation.

Even when 'free' the improvisation always operates within a chosen framework, otherwise the freedom that is produced is limitless and equivalent to chaos in nature or art.

The ideal movement class is a group of not less than eight and not more than twelve or fourteen participants. After each class, or once a week, there is a short evaluation period for free discussion of the work covered and queries raised. The fascination of this study lies in its disciplined freedom and its creativity.

20. Dance and Athletics

Dancers are both athletes and artists, and increasingly gymnasts and athletes find that dance classes are beneficial, if not necessary, to their work; and the relation between dance and skating needs no emphasis. One only has to look at such marvellous sporting performers as John Curry, Olga Korbut and Nadia Comenenci to understand what a great role modern dance and ballet plays in their training.

A perfect example of this is John Curry. As a young boy he wanted to become a dancer, but his father was against the idea and discouraged his son's interest in ballet. Consequently Curry turned to ice skating, and his father voiced no objections because it was, after all, a sport.

But as his training progressed he realised that the kind of skating he was interested in had more to do with art and ballet technique than with conventional forms of athleticism. By then he was old enough to make up his own mind about ballet training, with or without parental approval. He found a sympathetic ballet teacher and started taking classes, which he continues to this day.

The performances which won him the British, World and Olympic championship figure skating titles in 1976 owed as much to ballet as they did to conventional ice skating practice. Since then he has turned professional and in several West End shows has worked with ballet choreographers Kenneth MacMillan and Ronald Hynd and with modern choreographers Norman Maen and Twyla Tharp, among others, to transpose dance choreography to the ice skating stage.

John Curry is a determined young man intent on developing ice

skating as an art, and he is succeeding admirably.

This is only one example of the connection between dance and athletics.

In this country and in the United States experiments have taken place involving football players with ballet classes. At the end of a chosen period every football team, without exception, has had to acknowledge that the dancer's exercises both physically and mentally were infinitely more demanding than their own.

The ballet class, which through the years has transformed technique from a collection of French court dances into the scientific art it is today, has the power to extend considerably the original potential and mobility of any given set of muscles.

Who knows what limits will ever stop man's progress in the realm of movement, for each year we see athletes and gymnasts set astonishing new records and dance reaching out in exciting new directions. Dance and athletics thus share a seemingly limitless potential for pushing forward the frontiers of human endeavour.

21. Finale

Voltaire said 'Dancing is an art because it has rules'. And indeed the most effortless and natural looking dance – which seems to have been improvised on the spot – must have its own system or technique. Without these foundations, the result is the kind of free expression – run around the room doing whatever you feel spontaneously – which was rather popular early in this century but actually did no-one any good.

Self-expression is immensely important but can only be achieved through a set of rules. There are rules for putting letters together to make a word; for putting lines on a piece of paper to make a drawing; for putting colour on canvas to make a painting and for arranging notes of music to make a composition.

There is no way anything of value can be done without some framework. It might well be that the framework is discarded or the rules opposed, that is not important; what is essential is that they exist so that one knows when one is in opposition to them. It is not necessarily important that the rules be ideal or the framework perfect, not every system is right for every individual so one cannot say categorically only this or that method is correct. One can usually say what is best within one field – for example, in that of classical ballet dancing the most correct technique is best because it gives the most fluent and purest results, whereas exaggerations lead easily to acrobatic effects. Again, in acrobatics one notices at once the apparent lack of effort of the best technicians.

In whatever field of movement one works the complete appearance or illusion of 'freedom' is only achieved by maximum mastery of the technique. The technique of modern dance is mostly unforced, following the body's natural movement dynamics, but it still has its own system.

Whether it be the most difficult ballet step or the apparently most natural sway of the body it can only be done well if it is studied and mastered. Some teachers concentrate so fixedly on the very difficult mechanics that the pupil ends up with astonishing virtuosity but no idea of how to enter or leave the stage. Who hasn't seen a dancer finish a brilliant solo and then bow to the public like a scarecrow in the wind and walk off like a duck?

Art is not confined to great art, but is just as much the art of doing simple things very well.

Therefore it is always better to perform a minor role to perfection than to make a near miss of the principal part. The world of dance offers so many opportunities on different levels that there is a place for everyone who cares about it at all to participate. One can dance just for one's own enjoyment and satisfaction, or on stage for the enjoyment and satisfaction of others; or one can watch and appreciate or one can study aspects of dance historically and anthropologically. It is a question of discovering the area in which the greatest fulfilment lies, and that is by no means always the obvious one in the limelight.

Fulfilment comes with the knowledge of having given one's whole concentration to the project in hand and done it to the best of one's ability; that is the art of living. The magnitude of the job is not important for it is as difficult or more for an artist to paint a miniature as a large canvas. In other words, quality is more important than quantity. Quality is art, unrestrained quantity is vulgarity. What Voltaire said was simply that it is the rules that make the art.